Managing Your Money

Avant® Leadership Guide Series

Managing Your Money

A Lifetime Strategy for Financial Independence

George J. Mate

Avant Books®
San Marcos, California

Copyright © 1990 George J. Mate

All rights reserved. No part of this book may be reproduced or transmitted in any form or by any means, electronic or mechanical, including photocopying, recording or by any information storage and retrieval system without written permission from the copyright holder, except for the inclusion of brief quotes in a review.

Library of Congress Cataloging-in-Publication Data

Mate, George J.
Managing your money: a lifetime strategy for financial independence.

1. Finance, Personal.	I. Title.	II. Series.
HG179.M3469 1990	332.024—dc20	90-398

ISBN: 0-932238-50-5

Avant Books®
Slawson Communications, Inc.
165 Vallecitos de Oro
San Marcos, CA 92069

Printed in the United States

Interior design by Sandy Mewshaw
Cover design by Lorri Maida
Art by Estay Heustis

1 2 3 4 5 6 7 8 9 10

Table Of Contents

			Page
About the Author			vi
Introduction			vii

Part I
- Chapter 1 — Do It Right—Do It Yourself 1
- 2 — Back To Basics: Nine Doctrines 3
- 3 — Getting Started 9

Part II
- Chapter 4 — Assumptions and Principles 13
- 5 — The Investment Environment 17
- 6 — Investment Risk 21
- 7 — The Components 27
- 8 — Volatility and Dollar Cost Averaging 31
- 9 — Allocating Assets 39
- 10 — Mutual Fund Performance and Risk 43
- 11 — Choosing the Mutual Funds 47
- 12 — Your Personal Residence 51
- 13 — Mortgage Financing and Principal Prepayment Strategy 55

Part III
- Chapter 14 — Secondary Strategy: Enhancers 59
- 15 — Investments to Avoid 67
- 16 — *Vulture* Risk 71
- 17 — Tax Planning 77
- 18 — Insurance 81
- 19 — Retirement Planning 83
- Appendix I — Sample Financial Plan 87
- II — Basic Recommended Reading List 90
- III — Value of $10,000 Invested at 10% Compound Interest 92
- IV — Value of $1,000 Per Year Compounded Annually at 10% 93
- V — Secondary Strategy: Stock Market Valuation 94
- VI — Tax Deferral Advantage 95
- VII — Investment Net Worth/Asset Statement ... 96
- VIII — Term Life Insurance 102

About the Author

George J. Mate is a financial planner and a registered investment advisor. He is an associate of NAPFA (The National Association of Personal Financial Advisors), a professional organization of fee-only financial planners.

Mr. Mate was born and raised in Chicago, Illinois. He received a B.S. in Business Administration (Finance) from Northern Illinois University in 1969, and also studied Economics at Arizona State University. He moved to the San Francisco Bay area in 1972, and now resides in Oakland, California.

Introduction

Where can a person obtain the proper information needed to successfully manage personal finances?

Many turn to their junk mail advertisements and then purchase the expensive newsletters they read about, each promising a different road to riches. Some follow a strategy consisting of a random collection of various *hot tips* from friends and relatives. Some turn to financial consultants of brokerage houses or insurance companies and follow the free computerized financial plans they receive touting the company products. Others become disciples of *no money down* or foreclosure real estate gurus and begin dreaming of easy millions. Still others attend tax seminars and attempt to slash their taxes (while their net worth goes nowhere).

Brokerage house seminars eventually lead some to heavily commissioned and overpriced initial public offerings, complicated, illiquid, and expensive limited partnerships, etc.

Finally, some attend local college classes for less biased information on single subjects such as common stock or trust deed investing. They eventually learn that without a broad background to give them the big picture, a little knowledge is truly dangerous. They also find that practicality is often lacking in the academic approach.

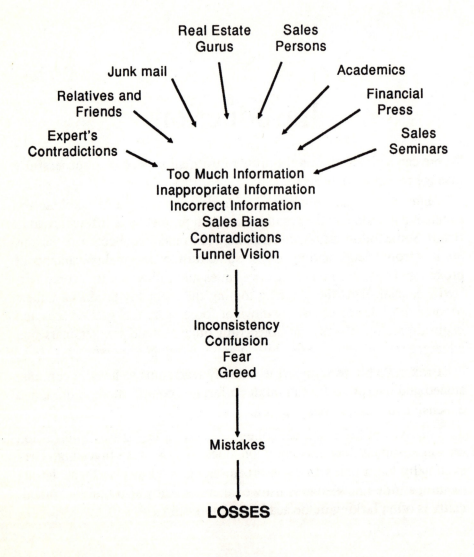

Figure I-1

Since most investors are constantly buffeted by crosswinds of contradictory information and self-serving advice (see Figure I-1), they cannot develop a concise long-term strategy and are doomed to failure.

To be successful in reaching objectives or goals, any person or organization must implement and follow a strategy with consistency. Personal financial goals are no exception.

The successful investment strategy:

1. Must be based on unbiased generic information.
2. Must be simple enough to adhere to indefinitely and to understand.
3. Must take into account the big picture of the complex domestic and world economy.
4. Should be an *all weather* strategy with some built-in flexibilities so that consistency can be maintained.
5. Must be practical so that it is attainable in the real, everyday world.
6. Must blend both risk and reward in a reasonable ratio.
7. Must take into account the personal, psychological, and financial profile of the individual.
8. Finally, it should allow the investor to fully control his or her own finances.

My long-term investment strategy meets these criteria. There is nothing complicated or mysterious about it. It will not provide exciting cocktail party gossip or instant riches. It is a practical, integrated, long-term approach that most investors can use to master their own finances, and build and preserve net worth, during the accumulation stages of youth and middle age. I call it my **money master** strategy.

x

Part I

Chapter 1

Do it Right—Do it Yourself

Some would lead you to believe that the small investor has no chance. They cite insider trading, brokerage house improprieties, market manipulation, volatility, and other reasons. I believe they are wrong.

The old saying, *If you want something done right, do it yourself*, has special meaning here. Before you throw in the towel, consider these points:

1. You have the powerful effect of long-term compounding working for you. Portfolio managers do not; they must emphasize short-term performance. You don't have to play this game. A 4% *real rate* of return should accomplish your goals long term.
2. Most large institutional investors have underperformed the stock market (Standard & Poors 500 stocks) for decades.
3. A select group of stock mutual funds are available that have beaten the S&P 500 consistently during the latest ten-year period using a buy and hold strategy. Many of these do not charge any sales fees. (See Chapter 11)
4. This professional management is generally available for a management fee of approximately 1% of assets.
5. Dollar-cost averaging of the aforementioned funds can provide a higher return than a *buy and hold*.

6. Once a basic program is in place, discipline and consistency are the traits needed to succeed. No special skills are required, the choice of securities is accomplished by the fund manager.
7. Government sponsored tax deferred accounts, Series EE U.S. Savings Bonds, and your personal residence offer *clean* ways to reduce and defer taxes.

Some people ask "Why should I bother to invest my money at 10% when a 6% inflation rate eats most of it up?"

Here's why: Lets say you started with a $10,000 lump sum.

After 20 years (with an inflation rate of 6%) it is worth only $3,115.

But, if during that time you achieve a 10% annual compound rate of return, your $10,000 becomes $67,275.

This $67,275 will be worth $20,958 in today's dollars. Thus the real value of the invested amount would be 6.73 times the real value of the non-invested amount. Assume the money is invested in a tax-deferred account.

Of course, past trends are no guarantee of future results, but the odds are in your favor. Take control and become the master of your money.

Chapter 2

Back to Basics

Many investors listen intently as the financial news media report(s) the significance of the inversion of the Treasury yield curve, the latest corporate leveraged buyout, or the evils of brokerage house arbitrage efforts. They listen as brokers attempt to sell them *unbundled stock units*, or a universal life insurance policy that is difficult to understand or compare to alternatives.

Much of the complexity in this modern world is necessary or even beneficial. Some of it, however, is unnecessary. Financial professionals can benefit from ever-increasing financial complexities, but it often clouds common sense and breeds confusion and dependency in investors.

For some investors with a large net worth and/or special situations, simplicity is elusive. Fortunately, in most cases, financial matters need not (and should not) be complex. My strategy emphasizes simplicity and practicality. It recognizes and incorporates simple and often forgotten ideas and doctrines such as the following:

1. **For most people, the critical part of the financial plan is a disciplined savings program.** It is difficult to build net worth without regular savings.

Studies have shown that persons of all income groups state that they find it difficult to save adequately. This would seem to indicate that people adapt to various spending levels. Anyone of any income group should save 10% of their income, including children on an allowance. A goal for aggressive, middle-income savers should be 25% or more of net income. Consider savings to be a debt owed yourself, and pay yourself first.

2. **A dollar saved by cutting expenses is more valuable than an earned dollar.** Usually, increasing your savings can be accomplished in only two ways: cutting expenses or increasing earnings. Cutting expenses is a more cost effective method since you get more for your money. You must earn an additional $1.33 or more to save one additional dollar. On the other hand, one hundred cents of every dollar saved by cutting expenses can be put to work since it was already taxed.

3. **You must concentrate on building net worth.** Every financial move you make must emphasize this idea. When making a comparison, or a choice, or analysis within your financial plan, the bottom line is, *How will it affect my net worth in the long run?*

   For example, what good is slashing your tax bill if it has a negative affect on your net worth?

4. **Debt is an expense.** Tax deductions only reduce the debt expense, they don't neutralize it.

5. **Depreciating assets and extra expenses reduce net worth. Acquisition of appreciating assets increases net worth.** Consider the following examples:

   If you scale down your taste in automobiles (especially the cost of a second car), you can free cash in the following manner:

   You could buy a brand new car for $15,000 using $6,000 cash and a four year loan of $9,000 at 12% interest. Four years later, you sell it for $6,500. New vehicles depreciate the most in the first two years or so. Your insurance cost is higher (in this case we will assume $600 a year higher). Your payment will be $237 per month for 48 months with a total of $11,376.

Interest expense is thus $2,376.

Cost: $ 6,000 Cash
       +11,376 Loan plus interest (non-deductible)
       $17,376
       + 2,400 Additional insurance expense
       $19,776
       - 6,500 Proceeds from sale of car
       $13,276 Cost over four years

Or, you could buy a used vehicle for $6,000 and sell it for $3,000 four years later:

$ 6,000 Purchase price
- 3,000 Proceeds
$ 3,000 Cost over four years

The cost in the first example was $13,276 and $3,000 in the second. The difference over four years is almost $10,000 (or $2,500 a year).

Now, lets say that you also decide to forego that one extra $60 dinner at the Hotel Costa Plente, and you only go there once a month instead of your usual twice. This frees another $720 per year.

$ 2,500 Year vehicle savings
+ 720   Year restaurant savings
$ 3,220 Year total savings

Let's discuss the significance of this $3,220 per year. Saving this $3,220 is the equivalent of earning approximately $4,285. Earning $4,285 nets approximately $3,220 after state and federal taxes. When tax rates go up (as they probably will), this factor will become more pronounced.

These are only two examples out of dozens of obvious ways to save. Pick one or two that you can live with and you can ignore the rest and still come out way ahead.

Investing an extra $3,220 per year for four years could easily yield $16,438 at the end of the four years. With no additional contribution, it could easily become $29,122 (or possibly much more) in six more years.

In the first case, (new car versus old car and one less extravagant dinner), you end up with nothing at the end of the period of time. In the second case, you have $16,438 in four years and over $29,000 in ten years. In the first case, you have bought a **depreciating** expense incurring asset and other expense items. In the second case, you have used the difference to purchase assets which **appreciate**.

To produce income other than salary in the future, **you must increase your net worth**. Increasing your net worth can be accomplished only by:

- Acquiring assets which **appreciate**.
- Minimizing assets which **depreciate**.
- Cutting expenses including debt.

6. **Money has time value and opportunity cost**.

    First remember that a dollar today is worth more than a dollar next year because of the erosion of inflation, and because it can immediately begin earning interest.

    Also keep in mind that, whenever a decision is made to spend or invest a sum of money, the alternative is interest at the current rate. The decision should reflect this *opportunity cost*, whether it is missed or exploited.

7. **The power of compound interest is truly astounding when given sufficient time**. Consider this example:

    Mary saves $150 per month and has done so for the past eighteen years. She does so easily, and it does not seem to hurt her standard of living. Charles, on the other hand, didn't begin saving until three years ago when he began to save $800 per month. This has been very difficult for him. Both have been earning an 8% annual compound rate of return in tax deferred accounts.

    Mary now has $72,803 in her account, while Charles has only $33,658. In fact, it will take Charles six more years of this *$800-per-month sacrifice* to catch up to Mary.

    Large returns are not necessary. The big difference was time and how it makes compound interest work. Moral to the story: Start early!

8. **Speculating is not investing**. A five-year U.S. Treasury note with a 9.5% yield to maturity is a proven investment. So is a blue chip

stock with a dependable ever-increasing dividend. Both have proven value.

What about an emerging growth stock such as a new small drug company with an untested product? The company has no proven value, unproven earnings, and pays no dividend. It is a speculation. The stock could soar someday, or become worthless.

Keep this difference in mind when you formulate your plan. Speculate only if you have some gambling instincts and then only with money you can afford to lose.

9. **Dollar-cost averaging is a simple and powerful tool.** It is examined in Chapters 7 and 8.

Chapter 3

Getting Started

There is no *quick cure* for financial problems, and there is no quick and easy road to riches. Reading a book or attending a seminar will not suffice. Reaching a specified financial goal or goals requires a specific plan of action as well as a permanent commitment of time, effort, patience, and discipline.

I recommend a five-step approach toward becoming your own money master:

1. Education.
2. Objective/Goal setting.
3. Developing a written financial plan.
4. Implementing the plan.
5. Monitoring.

The first step in the project is *education*. This book, as well as supplementary reading in Appendix II, can provide you with the necessary background to master your own finances. Without this background, you are at the mercy of others who do not always know, or care, what is best for you. Spend as much time as necessary in the education stage. My strategy can be implemented later, **at any time**. Put any investment ideas on hold; leave your money in a money market account. Disregard any and all advertising. If you want to be polite to the salespeople, tell them that they know it is improper to make investments without having a financial plan. If they have a proposal that *just can't wait*, hang up on them. Concurrently, during the education process, develop your own *financial profile* and put your objectives and goals in writing. Your spouse should be involved in the entire process.

Next, prepare a written financial plan including investments, tax planning, insurance, retirement planning, and estate planning. Consult a competent attorney for your estate planning. The plan should incorporate your objectives and goals and should include short, intermediate, and long-range planning. After the self-study period, some persons will be able to write the plan themselves. Others will need the help of a financial planner. I recommend a *fee-only* planner to avoid conflict of interest. They are scarce. The National Association of Personal Financial Advisors is a professional organization of fee-only planners. A list of members can be obtained by writing to: NAPFA, 1130 Lake Cook Road, Suite 105, Buffalo Grove, Illinois 60089.

Once your plan is written, implement it carefully in stages. Don't rush it. I have found that most people seem to feel they must hurry to *become fully invested* immediately or they feel they are wasting time or missing opportunities. Salespeople exploit this tendency, and costly mistakes are usually made. Worse yet, the investor never gets a chance to learn the patience and discipline necessary to make my program work.

Once the plan is implemented, set up a monitoring program as follows:

1. **Investment net worth update**

    Prepare a revised net worth statement at least annually. Calculate the total percentage change, taking into account any new money added. Also calculate any changes in percentages of assets by type. Do not include personal residence, vehicles, furniture, jewelry, etc. (See Appendix VII for detailed instructions.)

2. **Asset monitoring**

    Prepare separate file folders for each asset, including monthly statements.

3. **Tax records**

   Prepare a separate tax folder for receipts, etc.

4. **Residence**

   Prepare a separate folder. Obtain an amortization schedule for your mortgage loan, and keep records of any mortgage principal prepayments per your written plan. Save records of any capital improvements indefinitely.

5. **Financial plan**

   Keep the plan in a separate file and reread it at least every six months. Update the financial plan annually. No major revisions should be necessary unless a major *financial profile* change should occur such as a sudden disability or a major salary increase.

Once the monitoring program is set in place, approximately an hour per month should be all that is needed. In my basic investment strategy, asset accumulation is virtually on automatic pilot. Closer monitoring is required in my *secondary* strategy; as outlined in Chapter 14.

See Appendix I for a practical example of an abbreviated financial plan using my **money master** strategy.

Part II

Chapter 4

Assumptions & Principles

Will the stock market reach new highs this year, or will it crash again? What will the level of interest rates be late this year? When will the recession begin? Will we experience a banking panic, an oil price collapse, or maybe another strong round of inflation? What will new tax *reform* bring?

No one knows the answer to these and similar questions with certainty. In fact, if you follow the predictions of the economists, money managers, or newsletter writers for any extended period, you will find that they are usually contradictory, and that many are completely wrong as often as they are right. An article published in 1987 by the St. Louis Federal Reserve Bank claims that one could predict interest rates better than most big name economists simply by flipping a coin. In the August 8, 1988 issue of *Forbes*, columnist Ashley Bladen predicted that the United States would "follow the lead of the banana republics" and experience renewed accelerating inflation. Meanwhile, an adjoining column by Alan Reynolds claims that no renewed inflation is imminent as evidenced by continued declining commodity prices.

Various publications have for years been simultaneously predicting deflation, hyperinflation, and continued disinflation. Many are well documented and include convincing statistics to back each respective (contradictory) opinion and prediction. There is often disagreement as to whether we are in a *bull* or a *bear* stock market at a particular time. Who is one to believe?

The thing that really matters is how these factors influence the growth of your net worth. How can the average person with limited resources of time, money, and expertise, increase net worth despite an ever changing and unpredictable economic and market environment? By implementing and following a long-term investment strategy, which takes such factors into account.

My approach makes at least three assumptions:

1. Dealing with the complex financial world can be overwhelming. Simplifying matters as much as possible should be a key goal. Over the long haul, adherence is much more likely if the approach is direct and simple.
2. Consistent market *predictions* and *timing* are unlikely for the average person. They are usually out of reach of the professional, also.
3. A consistent long-term approach has the highest chance for success. The lure of the short term profit should be ignored with the bulk of your program. This approach may be construed as being boring, but finishing ahead in the long run is what matters. It is very difficult to stay on this type of course in this *quick fix* world.

The strategy that I recommend for most investors (with at least a portion of their assets) is very simple and straightforward. However, it is based on three principles which are often overlooked: *Controlling Risk, Emphasizing Compounding, and Emphasizing Clean Investments.*

1. **Controlling Risk** - Methods I use to control risk include:
    a. Several forms of diversification.
    b. Dollar-cost averaging to lower the average cost of your assets.
    c. Minimizing the use of leverage (it magnifies your profits, but also your losses).
    d. Avoidance of reactions to short term developments.

e. Keeping decisions consistent because all are made in the context of your written plan.
2. **Emphasizing Compounding** - It is the most powerful tool available to you, and is the cornerstone of my strategy.
3. **Emphasizing Clean Investments** - I refer to *clean* investments as those which minimize expenses (such as *load* fees, commissions, and high asset management fees), avoid the need for extensive record keeping, and avoid tax complications. *Clean* investments are also usually more simple in nature.

These assumptions and principles form the background for my basic long-term investment strategy.

Chapter 5

The Investment Environment

In order to take control and begin to plan a program, you should have some grasp of the following economic topics:
1. The United States economy and the business cycle.
2. Inflation, hyperinflation, disinflation, and deflation.
3. The United States banking system/Federal Reserve System/ monetary policy.
4. United States fiscal policy.
5. Interest rates and their cycles.
6. International economics.
7. Specific investment alternatives.
8. The influence of topics 1 through 7 on the investment alternatives.

A couple of months of self-study of these subjects (and others in this book) is essential to become a master of your money. Such knowledge can help to keep your program consistent if it is used to formulate your plan initially. The better your understanding of what you are doing, the more likely you are to stay on course. Here is an extremely simplified overview of the aforementioned topics:

The level of prosperity in our economy and the resultant economic conditions are determined by a complex set of factors. These factors interact simultaneously in numerous ways, and they result in a particular stage of the business cycle, interest rate level, flow of credit and bank reserves, level of inflation, level of employment etc.

International factors such as the price of oil, the prosperity level in other nations, and the international flow of credit have increased in significance in recent years. This has added to the level of complexity in the U.S. investment environment. The puzzle has become more complicated, and forecasting has become more difficult since global factors are so prominent.

At the risk of oversimplification, it can be said that all of the above factors create an investment environment that, at any one time, will fall into one of the following four categories (or a transition period between two of them):

1. **Stability**—During this type of period, the economy is growing, but not too quickly. Productivity is good, unemployment is at an acceptable level, interest rates are relatively stable, prices are rising very slowly, and no recession is imminent.

2. **Disinflation**—The rate of increase in the level of inflation has been dropping. Interest rates are, or will be in a downward trend.

3. **Deflation**—Prices have declined. Demand for credit is down. A recession is imminent or is in progress. Some areas of the economy are badly hurt, particularly in the real estate and energy sectors. There is a downward trend in interest rates. Bank and Savings and Loan failures usually increase, and there is talk of a *banking panic* and a deflationary *credit collapse.*

4. **Inflation**—Prices are rising at a quicker pace (in a hyperinflation they are rising drastically). The economy is growing *too quickly.* Credit has been expanded greatly, and sales of products of most types are soaring. Borrowers have to pay higher interest rates for the use of money and credit.

It is often difficult to ascertain which of these scenarios is current at any one time, since conflicting signals are often experienced. The increased influence of international factors makes this analysis even more challenging.

The individual investments within my strategy provide varied results depending on (in order of importance):

1. The perception of the public and private investors as to which aforementioned economic environment we are experiencing.
2. Which of the environments is actually in place.

It is extremely difficult to conclude with any certainty which of the environments is in place. It is even more difficult, if not impossible, to predict which environment lies ahead. Therefore, the only sensible strategy for most investors is to *hedge the bet* and position assets to cover all the environments. Remember that the first of the three principles on which I base my strategy is *Controlling Risk*. The first of five methods I use to control risk is several forms of diversification.

Diversification of assets by type is a defensive attempt to deal with the resulting problems of market change. David Dreman, author and money manager, discussed this subject in his October 28, 1985 column in *Forbes* magazine. He first describes various periods since the early 1900s in which various investments (and fortunes) triumphed and then crashed and burned. He concludes that "because the mainstay of our economy is change, the only reasonable answer is to diversify".

There are six investment types in my basic investment strategy. Most of these should be used in the basic program, thus providing diversification of type of asset (one of several forms of diversification):

1. Ownership of your **personal residence.**
2. **Money market mutual funds.**
3. No load diversified open-end **stock mutual funds.**
4. No load **bond mutual funds** (U.S. Govt.).
5. No load **balanced mutual funds** (as an alternative to 2 & 3).
6. **Series EE U.S. savings bonds.**

I will discuss these in detail in later chapters.

Chapter 6

Investment Risk

When it comes to money matters, your assets are **always** at risk in some form and to some degree, whether you buy real estate, put your money in the bank or stock market, or stuff it in your mattress. You can't eliminate risk, but controlling it should be a prominent part of your financial plan. Controlling risk is one of the three principles on which my *basic* strategy is structured. Failure to emphasize this principle can cause financial loss or catastrophe no matter where assets are placed.

In order to control the risk, you must first study what forms the risk can take. Various sources describe and categorize investment risk in different ways. I like to place it in these eight categories:

1. Market Risk
2. Interest Rate Risk
3. Business or *Credit* Risk
4. Inflation Risk
5. Deflation Risk
6. Liquidity Risk
7. Spending Risk
8. Tax Risk

Market Risk

Market risk involves the fluctuation of the value of assets as they are priced within their various markets (stock market, commodity market, real estate market, etc.) An obvious example is the stock market crash of October 19, 1987, in which most stocks lost a large portion of their value. From 1926-1986, (a sixty-year period) there were nineteen years in which an investor in the average United States stock would have suffered a net loss.

Recently, in the real estate market, owners of many homes, apartments, and commercial buildings in Texas suffered a loss of as much as 60% of the value of their properties.

In my *basic* strategy, I control **market risk** by several means:

1. Diversifying by type of asset, thus owning stock and bond mutual funds, money market funds, a primary residence, and possibly Series EE U.S. savings bonds. By owning several **types** of assets simultaneously, risk is spread, and the decline of any one market will be cushioned by stability (and possible gains) in other markets. *Balanced* mutual funds contain both stocks and bonds so they can be substituted for separate stock and bond mutual funds.

2. Diversification within asset or market category by use of mutual funds. A stock mutual fund can carry hundreds of individual stocks bought and sold by a professional money manager. This provides further diversification and helps control risk against fluctuation of individual stocks and fluctuation of industry segments.

3. Ideally, assets in each category should be purchased at the lowest possible prices. Since I feel that *market timing* should not be attempted at all in the *basic* program, I recommend dollar-cost averaging to help control market risk. See Chapters 7 and 8 for a discussion of this method.

4. I recommend totally ignoring short term economic and market developments in the basic strategy. The market crash of October 19th is an example of a short-term development which should not in any way change your strategy. In the basic plan, ignore economic forecasts and predictions, market *tips*, get rich quick

schemes, etc. Try to completely separate your emotions (such as fear, greed, and anxiety) from your program. This is the toughest part. The built-in mechanisms of my strategy, once you set them into place, will automatically take advantage of any values or bargains created by market fluctuations. The same mechanisms will automatically keep you from increasing purchases during an overpriced *runaway market*.

Interest Rate Risk

This is the risk of loss of the value of your assets due to changes in the level of interest rates. Interest rates are virtually always moving in a cycle. Sometimes they are almost stable, but usually are moving up or down with varying levels of acceleration or deacceleration. Interest rate changes affect various markets differently, but they have probably the most impact on the bond market. As rates go up, bond (and bond mutual fund) prices go down, and vice-versa. Bond prices dropped sharply in the spring of 1988 when interest rates rose suddenly. Most *experts* did not predict this event.

The investor using my basic program would not have been devastated by this short-term development, nor would he have changed his strategy at that time. He (she) would have been accumulating bond mutual shares prior to, during, and after this event using dollar-cost averaging. This program should continue indefinitely. Note that a bond mutual fund (as opposed to individual bonds) provides diversification within asset classification by including numerous individual bond issues in its portfolio.

If a *balanced* fund was being used instead, the same effect would be accomplished (but on a lesser scale), since the fund holds both stocks and bonds.

Another type of interest rate risk is re-investment risk. Investments that do not *lock in* an interest rate have re-investment risk since the future rate of earnings on this investment's returns are uncertain. If rates go down, less interest is earned in the future.

After the *basic* program is expanded, and United States Treasury notes and United States Treasury STRIP zero coupon bonds are included, interest rate risk can be reduced by holding several notes and bonds purchased at different intervals and maturities. More on this later.

Business Risk

(Also called *credit* risk or *capital risk*.) This is the risk of default by the company or business or municipality involved. Several years ago a major insurance company went bankrupt. Investors in this company's annuities took a beating.

Don't be misled by claims that annuities are *completely safe* investments. If an investor holds a large portion of assets in a policy issued by an insurance company which goes under, he or she can be devastated.

In recent years, some municipal bond holders in Washington state suffered losses in defaults. In many cases, insolvent Savings and Loans become credit risks to depositors. Also, when individual companies go bankrupt, stockholders become losers.

You can control such **business risk** by:
1. Avoiding individual stock, corporate bond, and municipal bond issues. (Use mutual funds instead).
2. Avoiding **large** investments in individual insurance companies via annuities.
3. Avoiding *junk* bond funds.

A sub-type of business risk is *event risk*. An example is the leveraged buyout of a company lowering the quality of its bonds. Avoid ownership of individual corporate bonds, and emphasize United States Treasury securities to protect against this risk.

Inflation Risk

This is the risk of a loss of purchasing power of the dollar in future years. No one knows for certain what future inflation levels will be. Avoid basic program changes in your strategy in response to news media *forecasts* of inflation.

In my basic program, building equity in your personal residence will help protect against inflation risk. Mortgage debt at reasonable levels at a moderate interest rate can help protect you against the unlikely occurrence of hyperinflation. As you expand the basic program via my secondary strategy in later years, gold mutual funds will add further protection against inflation risk, as well as add further diversification.

Deflation Risk

This is the opposite of inflation risk; it is the risk of paying back debts, or paying out future streams of income with dollars which have **increased** in purchasing power. A deflationary *credit collapse* would almost ensure such a scenario. Cash held in a money market, Series EE U.S. savings bonds, and bond mutual funds provide protection against deflation risk in the basic program. U.S. Treasury STRIP zero coupon bonds and U.S. Treasury notes can be added later for additional deflation risk protection (and all around diversification). A balanced plan to prepay your mortgage will also add deflation risk protection. Also, a variable rate mortgage would be beneficial during a deflationary period since interest rates would be pushed downward. (I'm not necessarily recommending a variable rate mortgage; however, the nature of your mortgage debt should be taken into account when you plan balance, diversification, and control of risk in your overall financial plan).

Liquidity Risk

This is the risk of having cash *tied up* and unavailable for cash needs or for new investment opportunities. A common example is the need for a down payment on a house. Don't plan on using proceeds from the sale of an investment for this or other large expenditures. Your *timing* will probably be wrong, forcing you to sell the investment at a loss. Part of your portfolio should be kept in a money market mutual fund, which provides total liquidity plus some income.

Spending Risk

This is a type of risk I have not seen discussed in financial publications. I consider it to be the opposite of liquidity risk. Having too much liquidity can increase risk by enlarging one's natural human tendency to engage in impulsive spending and improper investments.

Don't rely on your own untested discipline. Build it into the mechanics of your financial plan. Having a portion of your assets *frozen* into non-liquid accounts can be beneficial.

Tax Risk

A good example is the changes in the tax code concerning treatment of capital gains in the sale of assets. Many people (not just the rich) lost a lot of money simply due to a stroke of the pen by a fickle congress. Tax considerations in investment choices should be secondary. The six investment types in my basic strategy are *clean* investments that minimize tax risk and tax reporting complications.

Chapter 7

The Components

In Chapter 5, I presented the six components of my *basic* long-term investment strategy. I recommend use of all or most of these in your basic program. Let's take another look at them:

1. Ownership of your **personal residence.**
2. **Money market mutual funds.**
3. No load diversified open-end **stock mutual funds.**
4. No load **bond mutual funds** (U.S Govt.).
5. No load **balanced mutual funds** (as an alternative to 2 & 3).
6. **Series EE U.S. savings bonds.**

Why these investment types? The three investment types which have historically produced the best long-term returns (other than a personally owned business) are real estate and financial assets such as stocks and bonds. My choices emphasize these areas.

The eight types of risk are minimized in my program in four ways:

1. The nature of the choices.
2. The balanced use of all or most of the choices.
3. The method in which the assets are accumulated and held.

4. Consistency and discipline built into the program.

Real estate is owned in my basic program in the form of the personal residence. It is probably the most important asset, and should be purchased only after a careful search.

I use no-load mutual funds for the stock and bond purchases for many reasons:

1. They control business risk through diversification with hundreds of individual stocks and bonds.
2. They can be easily used in a dollar-cost averaging program, thus controlling market risk and interest rate risk.
3. They are *clean* investments which avoid unnecessary brokers' commissions, load fees, tax risk, and complications.
4. They are simple to buy, sell, understand, and track.
5. They are professionally managed.

The money market mutual fund is another important portion of my basic plan. It provides safety, liquidity, and a decent yield. There is no market or interest rate risk (except re-investment risk), and business risk is low. Inflation risk is relatively low, and the money market provides good deflation risk protection. *Spending* risk is high, however, since it is tempting to find *uses* for this money every time it has grown to a decent level.

Series EE U.S. Savings bonds are an optional component of the *basic* plan. They provide simplicity, safety, and a guaranteed decent yield. In fact, all U.S. Treasury Securities must provide a decent real return (above the rate of inflation) in order to attract investors willing to purchase them. The EE Savings Bonds return fluctuates, and is adjusted semi-annually at 85% of the rate on the five-year Treasury note. The savings bonds must be held five years or the guaranteed yield is lost.

Taxes on interest are deferred during the five-year period. There is no market risk, business risk, deflation risk, tax risk or spending risk with these securities; and inflation risk is relatively low. Interest rate risk consists only of *re-investment* risk since yields float and are not locked in.

My basic program eliminates trading or frequent selling. It is an accumulation program. It stresses buying, not selling. Assets are repositioned only at a much later stage in life. Emphasis is on timing the purchases, (not sales) via dollar-cost averaging. If the funds are dollar-cost averaged, they are purchased at a low enough average price to be held indefinitely until needed in the long-term financial plan. This allows time for compounding to occur. Compounding is the cornerstone of my basic strategy. In my basic program, dollar-cost averaging and compounding work hand-in-hand to produce good, long-term results. The funds are left alone; and dividends, interest, along with long-term increase in value provide the compounding one needs to produce the long-term increase in net worth. Selling and switching is usually a loser's game—and it is nonexistent in my basic program.

In Appendix III, you will find a 10% compound interest table. Note that at the end of ten years, a $10,000 investment has grown to $25,937. Five years later (15 years), it has grown to $41,772. At the end of 20 years, it is $67,275. In 25 years it is $108,347. This shows that the greatest power of compounding occurs after 15 years or so. Plan for a 15-20 year minimum in your program.

You can gradually accumulate the money market mutual fund shares and the optional Series EE U.S. savings bonds at any time since they have no market risk.

The stock and bond (or balanced) mutual funds present a high level of interest rate and market risk. Thus, the long-term purchases of these assets should be made at the lowest possible levels. I strongly believe that the most practical system for accomplishing this for most persons is dollar-cost averaging. I recommend its use for all stock and bond funds in the *basic* plan, whether they be in a tax-deferred or taxable account. Stock mutual fund shares are purchased at various prices during a market cycle in this program.

Bond funds fluctuate in value in an inverse relationship with interest rate changes or anticipation of such changes. Thus the dollar-cost averaging system works in a similar manner for bond funds (and *balanced* funds holding both stocks and bonds).

Larger amounts of shares purchased at lower prices will later snowball in value months or years later as prices rise in the inevitable next *bull* market. This means that patience is an absolute must.

Chapter 8

Volatility and Dollar-Cost Averaging

Many investors, constantly bombarded with information and advertising, are convinced that they must use forecasts and advice from various sources to somehow *time* the stock market and trade in and out of it. Although some investors have used such tactics to produce large gains, most end up with a widely divergent series of returns through the years ranging from big winners and good timing decisions to big losses from the inevitable timing mistakes.

I have prepared a hypothetical set of returns for a 20-year period depicting typical investment volatility in the following chart. Example 1 assumes an initial investment of $10,000.

Example 1:
Varied Returns (Market Timing Approach)

Year	Amount		Percent
1	$10,000	+	25%
2	12,500	+	25%
3	15,625	−	25%
4	11,719	+	8%
5	12,656	+	8%
6	13,669	+	20%
7	16,403	+	25%
8	20,503	−	25%
9	15,377	+	6%
10	16,300	+	18%
11	19,234	+	40%
12	26,928	−	26%
13	19,926	+	8%
14	21,521	+	10%
15	23,673	+	8%
16	25,566	+	8%
17	27,612	+	8%
18	29,821	+	8%
19	32,206	+	8%
20	34,783	+	8%
Total	$37,565		

Note that in Example 1 there are only three down years (25% loss in years three and eight, and a 26% loss in year twelve). There is a net gain in seventeen of the twenty years, including gains of 18%, 20%, 25%, and

40%. In the example, the investor finally tired of the volatility and settled for a steady 8% return for the last six years. He ended up with $37,565.

On the other hand, if he had *lowered his sights* and settled for a steady 8% return for each of the 20 years, he would have done much better and ended with $46,609.

If an investor purchased $10,000 worth of U.S. Treasury STRIP zero coupon bonds with a yield of 9%, he would automatically end up with $56,044 at the end of the twentieth year, with no risk.

Volatility is the enemy of compounding. As can be seen in the preceding example, **big losses in even one or two years can completely negate the strength of compounding**. If an investor sustains a 30% loss in one year, he must earn 43% the next year just to break even. That is no easy feat. Even if it is accomplished, one year's effect of compounding is lost. This will diminish the end result greatly unless several immediate years of successive large gains are accomplished.

Steady modest gains are automatically obtained with money market funds and U.S. Savings bonds as well as certificates of deposit and savings certificates. With stock and bond mutual funds, volatility is controlled via dollar-cost averaging. Look at the following examples which compare dollar-cost averaging to a buy and hold strategy in both a steadily rising and steadily falling market:

Example 2:
Dollar-Cost Averaging in a Steadily Falling Market

($100 Monthly Purchases)		
Month	Share Price	Shares Purchased
1	50	2.00
2	49	2.04
3	48	2.08
4	47	2.13
5	46	2.17
6	45	2.22
7	44	2.27
8	43	2.33
9	42	2.38
10	41	2.44
11	40	2.50
12	39	2.56
		27.12

Total shares purchased = 27.12 x $39 (ending Price) = $1058

Cost ($1200) - $1058 (ending Price) = $142 loss. Less $48 interest earned during period (at 8%) = $94 or **7.8%** loss

Example 3:
Buy and Hold Strategy in Steadily Falling Market

$1200 buys 24 shares at $50/share.

$39 = end of year price for a $264 or **22%** loss

Example 4:
Dollar-Cost Averaging in a Steadily Rising Market

Cost is $1200 over 12 months.

Ending share value is $50 during which time 27.12 shares are accumulated. 27.12 X $50 = $1356 + $48 interest earned = 1404 minus $1200 cost = $204 or **+ 17%** increase

Example 5:
Buy and Hold Strategy in a Steadily Rising Market

Shares price increases from $39 to $50. $1200 increases $338 to $1538 for a **28%** gain.

In Example 2, the share price falls steadily each month from $50 to $39. Column two shows that a monthly purchase of $100 buys an increasing amount of shares. Since the balance of the $1200 can be held in a money market fund all year, an average balance of $600 during the year earns $48 interest (at 8%).

Both gains and losses are *cushioned* with a dollar-cost averaging approach (17% vs. 28% gain in a rising market, and 7.8% loss vs. 22% loss in a falling market). **Gains are not as dramatic, but large losses are avoided**.

In my examples, both dividends and capital gain distributions were omitted for the sake of simplicity. Their presence enhances the moderating effect even further.

Dollar-cost averaging decreases volatility substantially. Since large returns are not necessary to make compounding work, but large losses defeat compounding (as shown in Example 1), dollar-cost averaging is the method of choice for the stock and bond mutual fund purchases in my basic program.

Dollar-cost averaging is based on a mathematics principle called the *harmonic mean* which is one of the methods of figuring averages. It guarantees that the average price paid per share in the mutual fund will be lower than the arithmetic average of the shares purchased. This is because the harmonic mean of a series of different values will always be below the arithmetic and geometric means.

It is outstanding in its simplicity, and is the closest thing to an automatic guarantee of good returns that I have found. It totally eliminates guesswork and the dangers of emotions such as fear and greed (and the accompanying losses they usually produce). It is difficult to accomplish, however, because it requires a tremendous amount of discipline. Most investors abandon their dollar-cost averaging program when prices are declining. This period is the most important time to buy in such a program.

Dollar-cost averaging does not, however, **guarantee** a profit to the investor. The danger lies at the point of sale.

Suppose you have accumulated $500,000 in financial assets at age sixty and are retiring. Part of the portfolio consists of three stock mutual funds accumulated by dollar-cost averaging over a twenty-year period. Imagine the year is 1987, and the funds have shown a decrease for the year averaging 10% due to the *crash*.

If you sell all shares at this point in order to reinvest for income, you will have defeated part of the dollar-cost averaging advantage. Attempting to time a lump sum sale is dangerous and often costly. Instead, simply end contributions and begin a program of regular periodic withdrawals from the stock mutual funds throughout your retirement. You will then be *dollar-cost averaging* your withdrawals at various price levels.

This withdrawal should consist of dividends from the stocks within the fund plus sales of selected shares of the funds. Consult your tax consultant at that time for the most advantageous choice of shares sold.

An additional point about dollar-cost averaging is the fact that it seems to work best with more volatile stock mutual funds. The reason for this is that higher levels of price volatility cause more frequent periods of lower prices during which shares are purchased. Thus, although volatility is the enemy of compounding, it can sometimes actually enhance dollar-cost averaging results.

Does this mean that investors should choose more volatile funds for the dollar-cost averaging programs? In my opinion, no. This strategy ignores the human psychological aspects. Price volatility can cause nervousness even in experienced investors. In newer investors, it will usually cause abandonment of the program, altogether.

As can be seen in Chapter 11, the stock mutual fund choices for my basic strategy have lower than average volatility. This is a *trade-off* which I feel is necessary for long-term success. Peace of mind is an important practical aspect of my strategy. A more volatile mutual fund stock can be chosen as part of my *secondary* strategy as described in Chapter 14.

In order to make dollar-cost averaging (or any investment program) work for you, you must first understand it completely and have faith in its potential. Carefully formulate a long-term program as part of an overall financial plan and vow to stay the course regardless of market conditions. The dollar-cost averaging program can be started at any time in the market cycles.

I have read and studied variations of strict dollar-cost averaging which are supposed to enhance and *fine tune* the basic concept. I do not recommend these approaches. As I said, the main advantage of the approach is simplicity. My basic plan incorporates basic human nature and psychology into its premises. (Psychological factors are missing in most investment approaches.) Complications decrease the likelihood of success. This *fine tuning* adds little return, but risks loss of the entire program.

Chapter 9

Allocating Assets

I showed how dollar-cost averaging reduces volatility for stock and bond mutual fund shareholders, and how this reduced volatility enhances the long-term effect of compounding in the framework of my basic investment strategy. Risk of loss from stock and bond price fluctuations are controlled by use of appropriate mutual funds, and by use of a long-term, dollar-cost averaging program. Separate stock and bond funds can be used or a *balanced* fund (which contains both stocks and bonds) can be substituted.

In accordance with a financial plan, the basic program should include an appropriate percentage of cash earmarked for a money market fund and a personal residence. What about additional money, if available?

I showed how steady *fixed* lower returns can produce superior long-term results. Then why include stocks at all? Over the long run, stocks **can** produce even better returns. But they will not do so unless two criteria are met:

1. Shares must be purchased at a suitable average price.
2. The stock mutual fund must provide at least average long-term performance.

Thus, I believe that some investors should completely eliminate stocks from their plans. These investors include:

1. Those who lack enough discipline to stick to a long-term program.
2. Those who will need the money in less than five to ten years.
3. Those who can tolerate no risk whatsoever.

Otherwise, investors should earmark any additional money for a stock or balanced fund and Series EE U.S. Savings Bonds. If a tax deferred, fixed income investment is available, it should be used in place of savings bonds, in most cases. These are usually an investment option within a company sponsored tax-deferred plan.

Also, investors who have purchased a primary residence can substitute a mortgage principal prepayment plan for some (or all) of the bond portion of the *allocation*. I will elaborate on this in Chapter 13.

Although flexibility should be built into your plan, the amount you choose for your mutual fund monthly investments should be relatively permanent. If in doubt, choose the lower amount so you don't have to cut back later and disturb the effect of dollar-cost averaging. Monthly deposits to the money market fund, savings certificates, and savings bonds can vary with no negative consequences.

How should one *allocate* between investments? This is a complex question and many individual factors should be considered on a case-by-case basis.

Younger investors, who already have purchased a primary residence, might best allocate new investment money each month within the following percentage ranges (older investors would vary the percentages):

Stock or *Balanced* mutual fund	50-80%
United States EE Savings Bonds	0-15%
Mortgage principal prepayment	0-25%
Money market fund	10-25%

Setting goals for percentages of total portfolio invested in various types of assets is called asset allocation. Adherence to these percentages accomplishes diversification by asset type as discussed in Chapter 6.

Many investors attempt an aggressive approach of changing asset type percentages in response to changes (or anticipated changes) in the investment environment which is described in Chapter 5.

For my basic program, I recommend a simpler and more practical approach. Simply set a goal for a fixed percentage in each asset category and set your monthly permanent investment amounts in each category accordingly.

Since your personal residence will most likely represent a disproportionate share of your assets in the first years of your program (and possibly even in later years), exclude it from your asset allocation percentages entirely. Calculate *financial assets* percentages only.

Typical pension fund portfolios use a traditional and relatively permanent allocation blend of approximately 60% stocks, 30% bonds, and 10% cash. This *60-30-10* blend is a time-tested allocation that has traditionally produced a respectable 4% *real* rate of return (4% above the inflation rate). This blend is ideal for my basic program.

Dollar-cost averaging will probably enhance your yield in the basic program since the pension funds are using a buy-and-hold approach (for the most part).

The *60-30-10* goal is merely a rough guideline. Don't modify your basic program by stepped up buying or premature selling (prior to retirement) just to obtain or sustain those percentages.

For example, suppose a thirty-year-old couple created a financial plan, purchased their personal residence and began my basic strategy one year ago. They chose a stock mutual fund over a balanced fund because they were also buying United States savings bonds and were making an extra monthly principal payment on their mortgage. (see Chapter 13).

They have been investing $400/month as follows:

Stock Mutual Fund $240/month	60%
United States EE Savings Bonds $60/month	15%
Mortgage principal prepayment $48/month	12%
Money market fund $52/month	13%

Thus, new money is being invested pretty much in line with the *60-30-10* blend.

Current financial asset totals and percentages are as follows:

Stocks	$2880	68%
Bonds	$ 720	17%
Money Market	$ 624	15%
	$4224	100%

Remember, mortgage principal prepayment will not be reflected in your totals ($576 paydown on principal). These figures will automatically adjust to a more appropriate allocation with continued dollar-cost averaging. Your goal in the basic program should be that 60-30-10 mix.

Later on, if a *secondary* program is started, additional *enhancers* can be added to serve a dual purpose.

1. To correct asset allocation imbalance and/or increase diversification.
2. To enhance overall yield of the portfolio. Secondary *enhancers* are described in Chapter 14.

Chapter 10

Mutual Fund Performance and Risk

Analysis of risk and how it relates to performance is sometimes a difficult concept to grasp. Reaching for higher returns in a fund usually means taking more risk due to increased market price fluctuations (volatility).

Before writing your financial plan, analyze your own tolerance for risk. Your anticipated *holding period* for your fund(s) must be defined when determining your risk tolerance. Time is actually one form of diversification since longer periods mean more variations in market levels. Over a long period of time, market fluctuations have less effect. Thus, younger investors can generally accept higher levels of risk. This risk can be varied in two ways when using my strategy:

1. **Asset allocation**

    Younger investors and/or those far from retirement can use the *60-30-10* mix with a 60% (or higher) stock mutual fund exposure in the basic program.

    Older investors should decrease the stock percentage in the allocation if just starting a basic program.

2. **Secondary strategy**

    Funds with a higher volatility can be used by investors with more risk tolerance in the secondary strategy.

As a general guideline, I consider ten years to be a minimum accumulation period for volatile funds. Even in the basic strategy, however, a longer accumulation period is favored over a shorter one.

Beta is a handy measure of stock mutual fund volatility. *The Individual Investors Guide to No Load Mutual Funds*, which is included in the Appendix II reading list, provides a good analysis of the concept of *beta* It also lists beta levels for 436 no load funds. Both Nicholas and Vanguard Wellington funds have a beta of .67 which is well below average stock market volatility of 1.0.

What can one expect to earn from these stock and balanced funds? Here are examples of past performance:

1. **Nicholas Fund**—A *long-term growth* stock mutual fund. From 1978-1988, it earned an *average annual total return* of 21.6% according to the *Forbes* 1988 annual mutual fund survey. A $10,000 investment in Nicholas at the beginning of this time period would have grown to approximately $61,000 after taxes at the end of the time period.

2. **Vanguard Wellington Fund**—A *balanced* fund holding both stocks and bonds in an approximate ratio of 65% to 35% respectively. Its *average annual total return* for 1978-1988 was 16.9% according to the same *Forbes* survey.

Why even consider a balanced fund like Wellington when Nicholas (and other funds) returned more? As discussed in Chapter 9, assets should be allocated to provide diversification and cut risk. A balanced fund contains both stocks and bonds and accomplishes this. You should think in terms of *risk adjusted performance*, measuring performance alone is misleading and dangerous. All of the mutual funds recommended for my basic program have good risk adjusted performance.

Should you choose a stock mutual fund or balanced mutual fund? Make your decision based on the following criteria:

1. Your age and *holding period*.
2. Your level of willingness to accept (and disregard) short term fluctuations.

3. Whether you have included other bond investments such as United States savings bonds or a bond mutual fund.
4. Whether you have included a mortgage principal prepayment program.

The stock market, as measured by the *Standard & Poors 500*, produced an average annual compound rate of return of 16.9% during the 1978-1988 period. However, this is unusually high for a ten-year period, and most stock mutual funds did not do as well. Historically, a 9-11% return is the norm for stocks. My point here is that unless you carefully pre-plan your strategy, choose the right fund(s), and follow dollar-cost averaging religiously, you will probably not even match that. Remember that 100% safe returns of 10% and more (periodically) are available in long-term United States Treasury securities.

You may know that you are unable to maintain a long-term program. Or, you may have only a short (five years or less) *holding period.* If so, avoid stocks completely and disregard the *60-30-10* guide.

For others, stock investments should be included in most portfolios. It is highly likely that my long-term basic program of stock mutual fund investing will produce a 12% average annual compound rate of return, and possibly much higher. This will offset the lower returns on other investments and provide good overall risk-adjusted returns with the entire portfolio.

I suggest a long-term goal of 10% average annual compound rate of return for your overall portfolio if you are using the *60-30-10* mix. This is conservative; results will vary. No guarantees of performance levels are expressed or implied anywhere in this program.

What about the relatively new so-called *asset allocation* funds? Most of these funds are nothing more than balanced funds which attempt to time the asset mix to changing economic conditions. As I showed in Chapter 5, this is an unrealistic goal. As I expected, most of these funds have performed poorly during their limited existence. A dollar-cost averaging program with your balanced fund should easily outperform their market timing attempts, especially on a risk-adjusted basis.

46

Chapter 11

Choosing Mutual Funds

Mutual funds are the *medium* I recommend for stock, bond, and *cash* investing. Here are four points to consider when choosing a mutual fund, ten characteristics I look for in funds, and my top choices in four categories of mutual funds for my basic long-term investment strategy.

There are currently more than 2700 mutual funds. Over 1000 of them are *no load* funds. At first glance, choosing a mutual fund from the huge amount of available choices seems an impossible task. But when my guidelines are applied, the list quickly shortens.

Remember these four points when choosing a mutual fund:

1. Choose a good long-term performer, but don't get hung up on performance comparison. **The average price at which you buy the shares is much more important than your choice of funds.** Instead, concentrate on your own performance in terms of discipline and consistency. Stick with your original choice and maintain your dollar-cost averaging program in your basic strategy.

2. For the most part, ignore performance comparisons of one year or less. Use three-, five-, and ten-year performance comparisons. This year's *winner* is often next year's loser. Don't try to guess which fund will top the lists in your basic program.

3. Exclude *aggressive* funds, sector funds, and *specialty* funds from your basic program.
4. Since stock mutual fund purchases must be long-term in the basic program, use any and all available tax deductible programs first (such as 401K's, deferred compensation plans, IRA's, etc.). Any *performance* advantages gained by choosing a fund *outside* of those available to you in deductible plans will be more than offset by lost tax advantages. These deductible plans should first be maximized before considering any other programs of stock mutual fund investing in taxable accounts.

I look for the following characteristics in the stock and bond mutual funds that I recommend in my basic strategy. Few, if any, *score* perfectly in all ten areas. I choose the fund(s) with the highest score.

1. The fund must be a true *no load* fund.
2. It must have operating expenses at or below 1%.
3. It must have a long-term average annual compound return of **over 16%** (to compensate for the additional risk of owning stocks).
4. It must have good **risk adjusted performance**. (See Chapter 10)
5. It must have had the same manager during the entire comparison period.
6. It does not use options or leverage.
7. It holds cash reserves for periods of heavy redemptions and/or purchase of stocks.
8. It has relatively low *portfolio turnover* (avoids excessive buying and selling).
9. Bond and balanced funds that keep junk bond holdings to a bare minimum.
10. It must be open to new investors and expected to remain so (to avoid a premature end to dollar-cost averaging).

With those criteria in mind, here are my choices of funds for my basic long-term investment strategy. They are listed by category. All are *open-end* funds.

Stock Mutual Funds

1. Nicholas Fund, 1-800-227-5987
2. Lindner Fund, 314-727-5305
3. Evergreen Fund, 1-800-235-0064
4. Vanguard Equity Income Fund, 1-800-662-7447

Balanced Mutual Funds

1. Vanguard Wellington Fund, 1-800-662-7447
2. Lindner Dividend Fund, 314-727-5305
3. Fidelity Puritan Fund, 1-800-544-6666

Bond Mutual Funds

1. Vanguard U.S. Treasury Bond Portfolio, 800-662-7447
2. Vanguard Short-Term Government Bond Fund, 800-662-7447

Money Market Mutual Funds

1. Vanguard Money Market Reserves Prime or Federal Portfolio, 800-662-7447
2. Kemper Money Market Portfolio, 800-621-1048
3. Capital Preservation Fund, 800-982-6150

Note that if you are eligible for a qualified tax deferred plan such as a 401K, 403B, etc., your choices may be limited by what is offered. In that case, choose the fund which scores the highest on my *characteristic checklist*.

I recommend the following supplementary reading to aid the investor in his mutual fund choices:
1. *Forbes Magazine, Annual Mutual Fund Survey* (Published annually in September)
2. *Individual Investor's Guide to No-Load Mutual Funds* Send $5.00 to: Mutual Fund Education Alliance, P.O. Box 11162, Chicago, IL 60711
3. *Handbook for No-Load Fund Investors* (annual) by Sheldon Jacobs. Send $38.00 to: The No-Load Fund Investor, P.O. Box 283, Hastings-on-Hudson, New York 10706

Chapter 12

The Personal Residence

Ownership of a personal residence is a key component of my basic long-term investment strategy. This chapter discusses the benefits of home ownership, the risks involved, and important decisions regarding the purchase.

For many investors, the personal residence is the only real estate asset owned or needed. In some ways it should be considered as an investment asset. However, emotional and other subjective factors play a large part in decisions regarding its purchase, improvements, and eventual sale. It is more than an asset—it is home.

For most persons, home ownership provides both intangible and tangible benefits. Intangible benefits include:

1. A sense of security and *roots*.
2. A sense of pride in ownership.

Tangible benefits include:

1. Steady (and sometimes spectacular) equity buildup (and resultant increase in net worth) with relatively low risk.
2. A *forced savings* program.
3. Important tax advantages.

4. A relatively low risk use of *leverage* (via the mortgage loan).
5. Powerful inflation protection.
6. Increased flexibility in future financial planning choices (increased credit, future tax planning choices, the possibility of rental income, retirement planning flexibility, etc.).

Most investors are aware of at least some of these advantages, but aren't aware of any of the risks. Since one important emphasis of my strategy is evaluation and control of risk, here are several types of risk regarding the personal residence:

1. **Liquidity Risk**:

    If the entire net worth is in the personal residence, and a large portion of the cash flow is needed for mortgage payments, nothing is left for other investments or sudden large expenditure needs.

2. **Business Risk**:

    If the monthly mortgage payment strains the investor each month, a sudden change of status or job loss can trigger default and loss of the home.

3. **Tax Risk**:

    The significant tax advantages of real estate should be considered *icing on the cake*. In their insatiable thirst for revenue to spend and votes to solicit, our lawmakers have shown themselves willing to change tax laws despite sudden (and sometimes disastrous) consequences for investors. For example, although some form of mortgage interest deduction will probably remain, the doctrine is under attack. *Nothing is sacred in the tax code.*

4. **Spending Risk**:

    If a large amount of equity has accumulated in a home, the homeowner is constantly tempted and pressured to spend excessively, via additional mortgage debt.

5. **Deflation Risk**:

    Last, but not least, a severe recession can *deflate* real estate prices sometimes quickly and dramatically. Although a severe deflation is unlikely, it is possible. Price declines of 5% to over 50% could result in any geographic area.

Most investors have been lulled into a false sense of complacency in this regard. They feel home prices can only go up. They often point to the fact that home prices in selected areas resisted any significant decline even in the somewhat severe recession of 1981.

They may be right. We may not see significant price declines of single family homes in certain selected areas in our lifetimes. Just remember, however, that *no trend lasts forever.*

In retrospect, the trend may possibly have ended in 1981 had interest rates continued to rise or had the recession lasted a while longer. It may have been *a close call.*

One *wild card* is the growing percentage of variable mortgages. If they had been as prevalent in 1981, we could have seen a much greater level of problems.

In his recent book, *Panic Proof Investing*, Gray Cardiff discusses his study of real estate cycles and claims that there have been regular ebbs and flows of fortune that have dominated our nations real estate markets for more than 150 years. Recent analysis showed that only 10% of San Francisco Bay Area households could qualify for a loan on a median-priced home in the area. Is the bubble ready to burst, or will we have decades more of the long-term upward trend in home prices? No one knows for sure. Just note the risks and do your best to control them.

There is no doubt that in many areas residential real estate is grossly overpriced in relation to other assets. On the other hand, the investor should always strive to buy value. Can you reconcile this dilemma? You must decide between buying, or waiting for lower prices which may or may not appear. Most choose to buy. Either choice, however, is a gamble.

What if you are *priced out* of the market, but still decide to buy? You have at least four choices:

1. Buy a *fixer upper* or a smaller property such as a condominium.
2. Choose a *fringe* area and plan on commuting.

3. Set up an *equity sharing* arrangement with a potential *housemate* or an investor.

4. Purchase a parcel of raw land now and build in the future.

Purchasing a *fixer upper* is riskier for obvious reasons. Condominiums are also riskier because of less demand and appreciation potential, as well as potential problems with the homeowner's association.

I have seen the equity sharing arrangement work to the benefit of both parties involved. In a typical arrangement an investor who is cash poor and/or has insufficient credit finds another to share various percentages of:

1. Down payment

2. Monthly mortgage payments

3. Interest deductions

4. Future equity

5. Maintenance/improvements

Numerous variations can be specified in a written contract based on the needs of each party in respect to the above components. It is difficult, however, to arrive at a fair deal for both parties because any advantage to either party can change in later years with changes in economic conditions or tax laws.

Chapter 13

Mortgage Financing and Principal Prepayment Strategy

Other important decisions need to be made including those regarding financing your residence.

First, should you choose a fixed or variable rate loan. The advantages of a fixed rate loan are:

1. Peace of mind.
2. Less inflation risk.
3. Ease of financial planning (no fluctuation in cost).

However, during the past five years or so, the variable-rate loan has proven to be more cost-effective for most, due to the interest rate scenario we have experienced. This could change in the future.

The investor must also make a decision on a fifteen-year or thirty-year loan, and whether to prepay the principal of the loan.

Shorter loans save huge amounts of interest expense. Here's why:

> Mortgage loan payments are based on an *amortization schedule* of the particular loan. A 30-year loan contains 360 payments. With each successive payment the principal portion increases and the interest portion decreases. Each month the borrower is paying

interest on the remainder of the principal as well as paying interest on interest. It is the exact opposite of an investment account earning compound interest for you; in this case it's compounding working against you.

Here's an example of cost differences:

Thirty-year loan: ($200,000 10¼% fixed rate)
Total interest cost: $445,200

Fifteen-year loan ($200,000 10¼% fixed rate)
Total interest cost: $186,900

The same savings can be accomplished with a 30-year loan if an extra principal payment is made each month. Which option is better? As usual, it depends:

Thirty-Year Loan Advantage:

You have more flexibility. If you are making a double principal payment each month and you suffer a financial hardship, you could cut back to a normal payment. With a fifteen year loan, you cannot.

Thirty-Year Loan Disadvantages:

It is very easy to abandon the *prepay plan* and spend the money on a vacation. The fifteen-year loan *forces* you to pay off the debt in half the time.

If you are paying a 10% compound rate of interest on your loan, prepaying principal gives you a guaranteed, risk free 10% compound rate of return on your money. The only difference is that instead of an instant cash return, you are getting a return in the form of future cost savings. Thus, it can be thought of as a sort of *quasi-bond* investment in the sense that you are locking in a fixed *yield* of future savings (if you eventually retire the mortgage).

To summarize, faster mortgage loan principal payment gives you faster ownership of your home, equity buildup, and interest expense savings. To get a better feel for the numbers involved, read *A Banker's*

Secret by Marc Eisenson. Send $4.95 to Good Advice Press, Box 78, Eligaville, N.Y. 12523 to obtain a copy.

How much, if any, of your available monthly cash flow should you allocate toward mortgage principal prepayment? Allocating **all** of it there adds risk by putting **all** of your net worth into your home thus violating the principle of diversification of assets. Each case should be analyzed separately using criteria such as:

1. Your financial *profile*.
2. Your goals.
3. The *age* and *terms* of your loan.
4. The level of inflation.
5. The rate of appreciation of your home's market value (How valuable is the *leverage* you are obtaining from your mortgage debt?) Remember, there was a long period in the 70s when having the largest loan possible was clearly advantageous.

Here are how just a few of the pertinent factors should affect your mortgage principal prepayment decisions when you devise your financial plan:

1. **Age of the loan**

    The newer the loan, the more interest expense you will save with each prepayment dollar. Assume you have a 9.25% 30-year fixed rate loan of $46,000. In the first year the total interest paid after 12 payments is $4,240, and the total principal paid is only $308. If, in the first month, you prepay the entire year's $308 principal payments, you save $3,886 in interest. Your next month's payment would be credited as the 13th installment payment (instead of the second). Now, you will also own your home free and clear one year sooner.

    If, on the other hand, at the end of the thirty-year mortgage, you prepaid the entire last year's principal payments of $4,066, you would save only $428 in interest. (In the last full year of payments, you are paying only $482 in interest.)

2. **The interest rate of your loan**

   Obviously, the higher the rate, the more favorable prepayment becomes since more interest expense is saved.

3. **The inflation rate**

   All other things considered, the higher the inflation rate, the less advantageous is prepayment of principal, because future dollar savings are worth increasingly less.

4. **Level of price appreciation of your residence**

   Principal prepayment becomes increasingly less advantageous as the level of price appreciation increases. If your home appreciated 30% in value last year, your 12% borrowed money has given you tremendous leverage.

5. **Whether you plan to remain in the home and *retire* the mortgage.**

   If you are in a *starter* home or don't plan on remaining in your residence and paying off your mortgage, I do not recommend prepaying any mortgage principal. The reason: If you sell prior to paying off the mortgage, you will merely retrieve your prepaid principal with no interest.

Part III

Chapter 14

Secondary Strategy: Enhancers

My basic investment strategy will build a solid base of assets from the six categories with a minimum of risk. For many investors, especially those with limited resources and/or limited time to monitor, the basic program is sufficient.

However, for those investors who have had a basic program in place for several years and have built such a base, the program can be enhanced with additional investments.

The secondary strategy is not a replacement for any portion of my basic strategy. The components of the basic strategy form the foundation, without which the entire program is exposed to unacceptably high levels of risk. In other words, don't purchase any *enhancer* investments until the basic portfolio is well established. This is especially true for the *miscellaneous* category listed in the example below:

Portfolio Enhancers

Primary Enhancers:

1. United States Treasury STRIP zero coupon bonds.
2. Additional no-load domestic stock mutual fund(s).

3. Gold-related assets.

Miscellaneous Enhancer Investments:

(To be used with a larger portfolio or special situations.)

    a. United States Treasury notes.
    b. Foreign stock mutual fund (no load).
    c. Real estate investment trusts (REITS).
    d. International bond fund (no load).
    e. U. S. Government securities bond fund (no load).
    f. Investment real estate (actively managed).
    g. Collectibles.
    h. GNMA mutual fund (no load).
    i. Annuity.
    j. Individual common stocks.
    k. Municipal bond mutual fund (no load).
    l. Closed-end stock funds.

The above example, lists three *Primary Enhancers* in rough order of importance, depending on your financial profile and other factors. Then listed are twelve *Miscellaneous Enhancers* that I recommend for investors with a larger net worth or with special situations.

If they are appropriate, the *Primary Enhancers* are recommended as additions throughout the years in approximate numerical order of priority. For example, I generally would not recommend purchase of gold-related assets prior to a zero coupon bond program. Nor would I normally recommend any *Miscellaneous Enhancer* in a portfolio containing just one stock mutual fund.

Each investment should be considered as a part of the whole portfolio rather than as a separate entity. Investments should compliment each other so that the portfolio remains diversified and does not become lopsided. As the portfolio expands, diversification can increase to include asset type, investments within asset type, maturity length within fixed income portions, etc.

Long-Term Investment Strategy Components

Basic Strategy Components

Personal Residence
Money Market Mutual Funds
Stock Mutual Funds
Bond Mutual Funds
Balanced Funds
Series EE U.S. Savings Bonds

Secondary Primary Enhancers

U.S. Treasury STRIP Zero Coupon Bonds
Additional Domestic Stock Mutual Funds (no load)
Gold Assets

Secondary Miscellaneous Enhancers

U.S. Treasury Notes
Foreign Stock Mutual Fund (no load)
Real Estate Investment Trusts REITS
International Bond Fund (no load)
U.S. Government Securities Bond Fund (no load)
Rental Real Estate
Collectibles
GNMA Mutual Fund (no load)
Annuity
Individual Stocks
Municipal Bond Fund (no load)
Closed End Stock Fund

Figure 14-1

As can be seen in Figure 14-1, the *Primary Enhancers* emphasize three investments, U.S. Treasury STRIP zero coupon bonds, an additional domestic stock mutual fund, and gold related assets. The purchase of U.S. Treasury STRIP zero coupon bonds should be first and foremost in most cases. These are not included in the basic strategy because they are a low risk investment only if purchased with an adequate yield to maturity and only if they are held until that maturity is reached. Many investors have a difficult time understanding what they are and how they work.

The best, and in most cases the only appropriate, place for U.S. Treasury STRIP zero coupon bonds is your IRA. I recommend committing your total IRA (up to a maximum of 20 percent of your entire investment net worth, excluding your residence) to U.S. Treasury STRIP zero coupon bonds unless you are within ten years of retirement. Use them only within a tax-deferred program like your IRA to avoid paying tax on income you are not receiving.

I recommend fully funding your IRA regardless of deductibility. In the long run, the tax-deferred growth advantage is far more important than the aspect of deductibility. Also, the advantages are significant even though non-deductible IRA's are not as *clean* due to increased accounting requirements. It is my opinion that U.S. Treasury STRIP zero coupon bonds belong in most investor's long-term portfolios. As shown previously, this bond with a 9 percent effective yield to maturity held in a tax deferred account can beat most other investments in ending value, especially on a risk-adjusted basis. The reason is consistent steady compounding at a guaranteed rate. Interest is automatically reinvested at the same 9 percent, regardless of the prevailing rate.

Open an IRA, or transfer an existing one, with a local discount broker (preferably one with no annual fee), who has the lowest commission rate, and the highest *effective yield to maturity* rate on the U.S. Treasury STRIP zero coupon bond. Target your maturity dates to age 59½ with each purchase. For example, at age 33, purchase a 26 or 27 year U.S. Treasury STRIP zero coupon bond.

You can use one of two strategies for purchasing your U.S. Treasury STRIP zero coupon bonds:

1. Purchase an equal amount through your discount broker each January for at least a ten-year period, thus accomplishing a sort of dollar-cost averaging program with varied levels of bond yields.

2. Hold cash in your discount brokerage IRA and make periodic increment purchases during periods of relatively high long-term rates. This program necessitates subjective decisions and educated guesses and requires a general knowledge of historic levels of interest rates as well as periodic monitoring.

The second most important enhancer in most cases is the addition of one or more stock mutual funds. When your first stock mutual fund (basic program) has grown to the $10,000 range, add a second fund and begin another dollar-cost averaging program. Almost all stock mutual funds in my basic program have a beta or volatility level which is lower than the market as a whole. You can choose another basic fund, a low cost index fund (like Vanguard Index Trust) with average volatility, or a more aggressive fund with more volatility.

For investors with large portfolios, knowledgeable investors, more aggressive investors, and those with more time and desire to monitor, a modified market-timing approach can be used with a portion of secondary money in an additional mutual fund. With this approach, I recommend increments of equal purchases during periods of relatively low market prices using such fundamental valuation gages as price/dividend and price/earnings ratios of the Standard & Poors 500, and average price/earnings ratios of the stock mutual fund(s) involved.

This requires additional independent study of valuation techniques (see Appendix V). Don't start such a program until and unless you already have substantial stock fund balances and you have the available monitoring time. Also, do not mingle this account with your dollar-cost averaged account in your basic strategy.

I do not feel that approaches in which 100 percent switches are made between stock and money market mutual funds are realistic. They turn out to be losers for many investors and are usually eventually abandoned for various reasons. Each *switch* requires two correct timing decisions in order to be successful (switching out and then back in again). This is very unlikely.

Gold-related assets are another major enhancer. I recommend using a no-load gold mining stock mutual fund such as Benham Gold Equities Index Fund.

Don't invest in gold-related assets until you have studied the gold market. I recommend timing purchases in a contrarian manner to coincide with depressed prices. Thus the best buying opportunities usually occur during stable or disinflationary times when there is little activity in the gold market and experts are declaring inflation dead. I recommend a modified dollar-cost averaging approach with the gold mutual fund (perhaps 12 equal monthly purchases).

Gold assets purchased in this manner should constitute only a small portion (approximately 5 percent) of your portfolio. They form a long-term hedge against inflation and should be sold only in the event that a severe inflationary period causes a very sharp rise in prices. Thus, they should be thought of as a sort of insurance policy.

Miscellaneous Enhancers listed in Figure 14-1, are appropriate only for investors with large portfolios, or for those with special situations.

Investors with very large portfolios should enhance or expand by adding some of them to further diversify and/or balance their portfolios.

In other cases, a special situation could call for use of one or more of the enhancers. For example, if an investor needed to fund a large debt or expense in the future, he/she could use a treasury note of the same maturity.

The note would pay a good return with no state tax liability and 100 percent safety, and would mature when needed if matched properly. Treasury Notes can be purchased with no fees, directly from the local Federal Reserve Bank.

Another example is an investor who does not want to own a personal residence. Real estate investment trusts could be purchased to give him/her some real estate exposure.

Note that these are growth strategies and do not pertain to retired income investors.

Here are some of my recommendations for *enhancer* mutual funds in my secondary investment strategy:

STOCK:
Vanguard Index Trust 800/662-7447
Acorn Fund 312/621-0630
Mathers Fund 800/926-3863
Twentieth Century Select (or Growth) . . .800/345-2021
Partners Fund 800/367-0770
Manhattan Fund 800/367-0770

MISCELLANEOUS:
Vanguard GNMA 800/662-7447
Vanguard World - International 800/662-7447
T. Roe Price International Bond 800/638-5660
Vanguard Intermediate Term
   Municipal Bond 800/662-7447
Benham Gold Equities Index
   Fund 800/982-6150

Chapter 15

Investments to Avoid

The six investment types of the basic strategy, the three primary enhancers and most of the miscellaneous enhancers of the secondary strategy, are *clean* investments. They have no load fees and their expenses are low. Most of them are simple in nature, easy to understand, monitor, and buy or sell. They allow you to retain control.

In the following example, I list my recommendations for investments to avoid:

1. Options
2. Commodities
3. Public limited partnerships
4. Universal life
5. Single premium life
6. *Load* and *hidden fee* mutual funds
7. Penny stocks
8. Initial Public Offerings (IPO's)

I recommend excluding them from almost any portfolio, either because they are too risky or they are not *clean* investments, or both.

1. **Options** - If used as speculation on future market price movements, they strongly resemble gambling. If used as insurance or a hedge against market price movements, in my opinion, they have not been proven to be cost effective. Also, both strategies lack simplicity.

2. **Commodities** - The vast majority of those who trade in commodities lose money.

3. **Public limited partnerships** - The success rate of these has been sporadic. Many investors have lost part or all of their investments. The risk/reward ratio is very poor. To add insult to injury, the brokers retain their large commissions and the management retains its usually large slice of the pie regardless of investor losses.

   There is virtually no liquidity with these products. There is no investor control. They are not clean investments; they are difficult to understand, track, and compare. Also, there are tax complications as well as tax risk due to constant tax law changes. They are an accounting nightmare. If these are not enough reasons, the K-1 IRS statements needed for filing taxes are often sent too late to file without an extension: Forget public limited partnerships entirely.

4. **Universal and Single Premium Life Insurance** - As with public limited partnerships, these products make life unnecessarily more complicated for the investor. They force the investor to merge life insurance protection with investments. It then becomes difficult to make comparisons, shop aggressively, or monitor performance. I have found that separate purchases of term insurance and investments is almost always more cost effective. It also allows the investor to retain more control.

   Tax advantages in these investments are often exaggerated by salespeople and the tax risk is not explained. This risk stems from the fact that changes in future tax laws can suddenly negate some of the positive features of these investments and make them instant losers. Any positive features are outweighed by the negatives, which include lack of liquidity.

5. **Load Mutual Funds** - Salespeople will give you a dozen reasons to buy them. Some reasons are misleading and the rest are downright false. Study after study has shown there is absolutely **no** performance advantage in load funds. Load fees are wasted money.
6. **Penny Stocks** - It is extremely difficult to obtain accurate, unbiased information on these issues. Although a small percentage of these stocks skyrocket in value, the odds are very slim. Fraud is common. Costs are very high because the investor not only pays an odd lot commission, but also a spread between bid and asked price. The spread can be very large with these thinly traded issues.
7. **Initial Public Offerings (IPO's)** - These are usually some type of closed-end funds that will trade on an exchange. They are aggressively marketed by brokers who earn a generous commission on them. The problem is that they are usually priced too high initially, and the price usually goes down after they are traded.

For obvious reasons, the products listed above are pushed the hardest by salespeople. False and misleading claims and comparisons are constantly made. Here are some of the more common ones:

1. Downplaying the risk involved in safe commodity and option strategies.
2. False claims of long-term high performance in *other* clients' options/commodities accounts. (The *real* proof is actual inspection of the clients' IRS returns.)
3. Artificially high term life quotes used by brokers in sales comparisons with single premium life and universal life.
4. Failure to point out hidden fees and charges in limited partnerships and life insurance products.
5. Misleading and incorrect claims regarding inherent tax risk and tax complications with limited partnership and insurance products.
6. Misleading tax advantage claims: Tax deferral can be accomplished with IRA's and other government-sponsored plans, and these should be fully funded first. Any additional deferral can be accomplished with annuities which are less complicated than single premium life (and usually less costly).

7. Misleading claims of high, safe rates of return: Rates of return on fixed income investments are determined by the market and reflect the inherent level of risk. Rates on 100% safe U.S. Treasury securities can be used as a handy benchmark comparison. If current 10-year U.S. treasury note rates are 8% and a salesperson claims to have a product offering a safe 10% fixed rate for 10 years, something is wrong. Common techniques used to inflate yields include using low quality *junk* bonds, returning principal as part of the yield, and/or using options strategies to enhance yield. All three increase risk.

8. Misleading performance data based on selective time periods or varied time parameters of investment products.

9. Confusing the terms *sales load* and *management fee*. **All** stock mutual funds have management fees (which average approximately 1%). However, no-load funds have **no sales load whatsoever**. Sales loads of 1% to 9% are imposed on some funds **in addition** to management fees. All of this sales load goes into the broker's pocket. None is used to manage the fund.

10. Misleading claims of *load* fund performance. I have seen brokers use selected time period comparisons which are misleading. Always compare apples to apples. Insist on 3-, 5-, and 10-year comparisons, using sources described in Chapter 11, *Choosing a Mutual Fund*.

Retain control of your finances by sticking to the solid and simple investments recommended in my basic and secondary strategies. You will come out ahead in the long run with a lot fewer headaches and greater control.

Chapter 16

Vulture Risk

Sandra is a 36-year-old salesperson. She is single and has a good salary. She had $50,000 equity in her condominium and had cash and investments worth $60,000. Two years later, her net worth had shrunk from $110,000 to $10,000, and she was working a second job to pay for her new second mortgage payments.

Al is a 45-year-old police officer. He had been married 18 years and had two young children. His wife lost her job and had not worked the past eight years. However, his steady income and some careful planning built an investment portfolio of $76,000. He had been looking forward to a 50% pension in just five years. The couple had owned their home for 11 years and had paid down their mortgage to only $30,000, giving them $200,000 equity in their home.

One year later, Al was living alone in a small apartment. His share of the marital assets (excluding his pension) had been $138,000. Unbelievably, this would soon shrink to only $15,000. He was now working a second job to pay $1500/mo. to his ex-spouse. Since they had a long-term marriage, $900 of that payment could last indefinitely and could increase in the future. Although he still had 100% of his pension interest, his retirement would be delayed indefinitely.

Joe and Anne are a 71-year-old retired couple. As a supplement to their small $1100 per month social security benefits, a broker recommended that they place their $100,000 life savings in a *solid* public real estate limited partnership that he said would generate income and protect them against inflation. Two years later, the partnership was deeply in trouble and suspended its dividend payments. They don't know how much, if any, of their life savings will be recovered.

In all three of these examples (which are based on fact), years were spent building a financial base only to have a sudden financial catastrophe destroy the results of much hard work and planning. Similar situations occur constantly.

These hardships are caused by the actions of people whom I consider to be *vultures*. They legally exploit others who have managed to accumulate a net worth. There are scores of salespeople, lawyers, ex-spouses, and malcontents, who are ready, willing, and able to go after other peoples' assets, including yours. This risk must be understood and steps taken to protect against it. I call it *vulture* risk. Let's examine the circumstances in the three examples I gave:

In Sandra's case, she was involved in a traffic accident resulting in injuries to a pedestrian who was partly responsible for the accident. The pedestrian claimed permanent disability and was awarded a large settlement. Since Sandra was carrying only minimum auto liability, the difference came from her assets. She estimates that it will take ten years to regain what was lost.

Al certainly fared no better. As a result of his divorce, he lost his home and most of his assets. He will **never** recover. As part of his settlement agreement, he found that his debts were as follows:

1. $79,000 - Ex-spouse's interest in pension
2. 38,000 - Ex-spouse's interest in joint accounts
3. 5,000 - His attorney fees
4. 5,000 - Her attorney fees
5. 5,000 - Additional miscellaneous expenses
6. 1,500 - per month alimony and child support

Here's how the assets were divided:

1. The house was sold for $230,000 and netted $91,000 to each spouse after expenses.
2. His wife was awarded a 36% interest in his pension. An actuarial study valued the pension at $220,000 because of the anticipated lifetime growing stream of income. Her interest was thus valued at $79,000.
3. The joint investment accounts were sold (which generated additional tax liabilities). His $38,000 interest in them was used to partially offset the pension interest. The difference came from his share of the house sale.
4. He was ordered to pay her attorney fees.
5. He was ordered to pay $600 per month child support.
6. He was ordered to pay $900 per month in spousal support. Since it was a long-term marriage, the support was open-ended and **could** last her entire lifetime, provided she did not remarry.

Calculations:

$91,000	Sale of house
(10,000)	Attorney Fees
(5,000)	Additional expenses & purchases.
+38,000	Credit for his share of joint accounts
(79,000)	Interest in pension owed to spouse
$35,000	

Since he could not qualify for a new loan and did not want a condominium, he faced loss of another $20,000 for his share of capital gains tax on the sale of the house. This would leave him with only $15,000.

In my opinion the following are basic causes of *vulture* risk:

1. **Conflict of interest inherent in the work of civil attorneys.**

Attorneys can make more money when civil cases are contested. Therefore, they cannot be counted on to handle cases efficiently. This conflict of interest can cause attorneys to encourage discord between plaintiff and defendant because it is often profitable for them to do so. It costs clients dearly and it is also an incredible waste of resources.

There are more attorneys in one state (California) than in many countries in the world. In every state, some of them prey on human greed, and do so with impunity in a seemingly unregulated environment. Litigation permeates our society, much of it unproductive and frivolous.

2. **Conflict of interest inherent in selling financial products.**

Many financial advisors, who make commissions from products they recommend, succumb to temptation and sell inappropriate and often risky financial products with no regard for the customers' interests. There is usually no recourse after the resulting catastrophe.

3. **Subjective and unfair civil laws and/or subjective and unfair interpretations of them.**

How can you protect against *vulture* risk? It cannot be eliminated, but it can be controlled to some degree by increasing your knowledge and taking a few precautions.

Many large awards granted to civil plaintiffs are grossly out of line with common sense. Adequate insurance coverage is an absolute necessity. If you have substantial assets, purchase a one or two million dollar umbrella policy to enhance your automobile and homeowner's liability. Do your best to avoid uninsured litigation, and be aware of conflicts of interest when dealing with attorneys.

Knowledge is your best defense against financial sales *vultures*. Educate yourself in financial matters, devise your financial plan (or have one written for you), and **manage your own money**. Then, in the context of your knowledge and your written plan, improper proposals will be recognized.

Divorce *vulture* risk is a more complicated and emotional issue. It is more difficult both to understand and to protect against.

Civil case law regarding a spouse's interest in his/her spouse's defined benefit plan (pension) was intended to protect the property rights of the nonpensioned spouse. To many people, this entire concept is inherently unfair. But what often makes it disastrous for the pensioned spouse is the artificially inflated value placed on the future benefits due to *actuarial studies*.

If you doubt that the process can defy common sense, consider this: Imagine yourself expecting to receive your pension benefits just prior to retirement. Your spouse divorces you and is awarded half your pension, which is valued at $200,000. Your choices are: (1) Receiving only half of your normal monthly benefit at retirement. (2) Relinquishing your right to other assets worth $100,000.

You **may** not even be given a choice since the court could (under certain circumstances in some states) choose No. 2 for you. This is, of course, **in addition** to any other assets such as half interest in home equity, joint accounts, deferred compensation, 401K's, support, etc. The result is sometimes irreversible financial catastrophe.

No one thinks it could happen to them. "My spouse would never do that," they say. Unfortunately, many *victims* have had the same confidence. They now know better.

Although there is no absolute protection against this type of risk, the following measures can provide some protection:

1. Documentation should be made of respective assets and net worth at the time of marriage.
2. A detailed, fair, professionally prepared prenuptial agreement enacted **prior** to marriage can be written. Both parties should be represented by attorneys, and extra signed, notarized copies should be held at their offices. In the agreement, many issues can be dealt with such as defined benefit (pension) rights, open-ended support, etc.
3. The spouses should keep financial records providing a *paper trail* of respective assets.

A prenuptial is not for everyone. It can create a climate with a *self-fulfilling prophecy*. Also, as a legal document, it **will** be attacked by the spouse's attorney, thus encouraging additional attorney *vulture* risk. In some cases, prenuptials have, however, protected against financial catastrophe. Understand the issues before making your decision.

Chapter 17

Tax Planning

Most of this book has dealt with my long-term investment strategy which is designed to build and preserve net worth. My *basic* strategy strongly discourages *shifts* in response to economic and market changes, new tax laws, and changes in one's individual perceptions and emotions. Although some modifications are necessary from time to time, they should be accomplished within the framework of some built-in flexibilities in the financial plan.

Traditionally, tax planning has been done in conjunction with investment strategy planning. This causes a dilemma. How can the investor merge long-term investment planning with tax planning when the United States tax code has become a three-ring circus? There seems to be no stability or consistency in the tax code with new tax legislation being proposed or enacted every year.

This schizophrenia is a bonanza for tax accountants and also for brokers who can justify recommendations for constant shifting of investments in response to the tax changes.

A more sensible approach is to first attempt to identify those few consistent *themes* within the tax code that seem to have staying power. The two obvious ones are:

1. The preferential treatment of real estate investments.
2. The preferential treatment of government-sponsored retirement and savings plans.

Once they are identified, the investor should follow a long-term investment strategy that takes these ever-present themes into account and fully exploits them. When written into the financial plan, such a strategy will keep the investor on a steady course and shield him/her from sales pressures for unnecessary, costly, and destructive changes.

It is probably safe to assume that some sort of preferential tax treatment for real estate will remain whether it be mortgage interest deductions, deferral of capital gains tax on sale of personal residence, the over 55 years of age exclusion, or all of these. Thus, ownership of your personal residence is the most obvious example of merging tax and investment planning on a *permanent* basis. Also, for some investors with large portfolios, investment real estate may be suitable. Up to $25,000 of losses from actively managed rentals can be used to reduce taxable income in many cases.

I recommend funding any and all available tax deferred savings/retirement plans to the maximum with any available long-term money. Even non-deductible IRA's should be maximized (see Appendix VI). Don't use money you will need prior to retirement, however.

In the beginning, when taxable accounts are small, the tax bite is not noticeable. However, when a taxable investment account has grown to a sizeable amount, it really begins to hurt. A $30,000 taxable money market account earning 9% interest (or $2700 per year) will add approximately $890 to your yearly tax bill. The same $30,000 balance in an IRA adds no yearly taxes, of course.

When planning your asset allocation, a decision on a choice between a pure stock mutual fund versus a balanced fund is influenced by the availability (or unavailability) of a government sponsored tax deferred account such as a 401K plan at your place of employment. Specifically, the additional income generated from bonds within a balanced fund are worth less in a taxable account.

The case for both annuities and municipal bond mutual funds is not as obvious. Note that I recommend them only in the Miscellaneous Category of my secondary strategy. They are suitable for only some investors with large portfolios and/or special situations.

If an investor with a large portfolio has fully funded all available qualified tax deferred plans and still has more than ten years until retirement, an annuity **may** be appropriate for a portion of assets in **some** cases. Keep in mind the disadvantages, however. There is the *tax risk* of the possibility of future repeal of tax deferred status as well as lost liquidity and *credit risk* of the insurance company. These are added expenses, also.

Municipal bond mutual funds are another puzzle. It is often questionable whether these are advantageous for investors. There is a large amount of interest rate risk, and some credit risk. When these yields are the same as, or only slightly above, other available after-tax yields, they lose appeal. Interest rate risk, liquidity risk, and credit risk can be controlled to some degree using municipal bond funds (instead of individual issues) and by using dollar-cost averaging.

Despite new restrictions on shifting income to children (kiddie tax) to lower taxes, the first $500 of income from an investment in the child's name is exempt from taxes and the second $500 is taxed at the lowest rate. This applies to children under 14 years-of-age. However, investment accounts in the child's name which generate over $1000 income are taxed at the parents highest rate. Set up these accounts accordingly. Also, interest from U.S. Savings Bonds (series EE), purchased after January, 1990, is tax free (not just deferred), if used for educational purposes, (in many cases).

As a final word on tax planning, I recommend monitoring your withholding of tax from earned income. Estimate your year-end federal tax bill and attempt to *break even* by dividing the estimated total by the number of pay periods and then withholding that amount. Estimate on the plus side to avoid penalties. Some people like to withhold much more than necessary as a form of forced savings. This practice is unsound because the *savings* is really an interest-free loan to the government.

Chapter 18

Insurance

Since there are already many excellent sources available on risk management, I'll touch on this subject only briefly. Also, since the main subject of this book is long-term investment strategy, I will forego analysis of life insurance needs. Life insurance could more suitably be called *death insurance* since it's primary purpose should be to replace the stream of income provided by the person insured. It is essential to estate planning. I recommend using term insurance. Purchase the lowest cost term policy available from an A or A+ company (rated by A.M. Best) at a level commensurate with the family's income levels, age, net worth, and other factors.

In some cases, an even more critical component is disability insurance. If the breadwinner(s) become disabled and cannot work, an even worse situation develops since the former breadwinner(s) must now also be supported.

If term life and/or disability insurance is called for in your individual situation, shop aggressively and use the A or A+ company with the best deal.

In your analysis, don't rely on a salesman's estimates of your insurance needs. As part of your self-management program of your financial plan, research the matter yourself and include insurance planning in your written financial plan. There are many excellent books available with sections devoted to risk management or insurance planning. Also, many of the numerous consumer financial periodicals often contain worksheets and other data on calculating insurance needs. Analyze your situation and act accordingly.

Chapter 19

Retirement Planning

When developing your financial plan, you must attempt to calculate income needs at retirement, and calculate how large your investment net worth must be to provide the proper income stream.

Several assumptions must be made, so remember your figures will be only rough estimates. These assumptions include:

1. Future income needs.
2. Future rate of inflation.
3. Future investment returns.
4. Possibility of interim disabilities.
5. Your interim income levels.

Your *lump sum* investment net worth at the time of retirement can provide a relatively fixed stream of income. However, income needs rise each year with cost of living increases. Some of your income may rise with inflation such as rental income, Social Security income, stock mutual fund dividend income, and some types of pension income.

These factors sometimes make it difficult to accomplish retirement planning, and you may wish to consult a financial planner for assistance.

There are numerous books available on retirement planning. They provide charts and worksheets which can be helpful.

You may wish to purchase and learn to use a business calculator. The accompanying manuals will show how to use the machine and produce the calculations necessary for retirement planning. You can then prepare a year-by-year analysis of anticipated total annual retirement income, anticipated annual required income, and resulting annual surplus or deficit. Some new computer software also does this.

To obtain an estimate of your future social security benefit, call your local Social Security office and ask for form SSA-7004-PC-OP2. Complete and mail in the form.

Unless you estimate your income needs in retirement in detail, use 75-90% of current income as a rough guide. Remember that you may no longer have a mortgage payment.

As I stated, assumptions regarding variables have to be made. I use the following assumptions for the following reasons:

1. **5% inflation rate**. Inflation as measured by the Consumer Price Index has averaged 4-5% for the past several years. For a relatively brief period, it was much higher. However, the historical norm is closer to 3%.

2. **10% compound annual rate of return (during accumulation period)**. See Chapter 10.

3. **8% compound annual return during withdrawal period**. It may be prudent to replace **some** of your more volatile assets (such as a long term bond mutual fund or a stock mutual fund with a high beta) with U.S. Treasury notes, Certificates of Deposit, or a low beta stock fund during the withdrawal phase. This would reduce your overall return.

As an example, let's say you will need $35,000 of income at retirement (in today's dollars). You expect to receive $17,000 per year pension and/or social security benefits that first year. Thus you will need to generate $18,000 in income from investments (in today's dollars) for the first year of retirement.

Simple, rough estimates can be made using the following factors and calculations:

1. Assume a 5% average annual inflation rate. Use the factors 1.28, 1.63, 2.08, and 2.65 for 5, 10, 15 and 20 years respectively to calculate inflation's effect. For example, $18,000 today will require $18,000 x 2.65 or $47,700 twenty years from now. Also, a pension with a $17,000 annual benefit today will pay out $45,050 (17,000 x 2.65) as an annual benefit 20 years from now (provided the amount grows by an average annual 5% rate).

2. You will need a lump sum when you retire to make the periodic withdrawals which you will need for the rest of your life. Assume an 8% annual compound rate of return after retirement on your accumulated lump sum. Use the factors 9.2, 10.6, 11.5, and 12.5 to calculate what lump sum is needed to generate a particular income stream for 15, 20, 25 years, and for an **indefinite** period (respectively). Multiply the factor by the required annual income stream to obtain the necessary lump sum. For example, to generate $47,700 annually for an indefinite period (forever), you will need $47,700 x 12.5 or $596,250 in 20 years.

3. To calculate what annual investment amount is needed to generate this lump sum of $596,250, simply divide by the appropriate factor from the following chart: (10% annual compound return).

Years to Retirement	Factor	(@ 10% annual compound return)
10	17.53	
15	34.95	
20	63.00	
25	108.18	

For example, to generate a lump sum of $596,250 in 20 years, you need to invest $596,250 divided by 63 or approximately $9,464 per year or $788 per month.

4. What if you already have accumulated a $25,000 sum? Calculate as follows, adding a step:

- Step 1

  Calculate the future value of your current amount, assuming a 10% annual compound return.

Years to Retirement	Factor
10	2.59
15	4.17
20	6.73
25	10.83

  $25,000 x 6.73 = $168,000

- Step 2

  Subtracted from the lump sum you'll need:

  $596,250
  <u>-168,250</u>
  $428,000

- Step 3

  Now calculate what annual investment amount is needed to raise this smaller lump sum, continuing to use the factor of 63 (10% annual compound return at 20 years to retirement):

  $428,000 x 63 = $6794 per year or $566 per month

These calculations assume investment within tax deferred accounts, or taxes paid separately from additional money. Remember, these amounts will become inadequate quickly unless annual increases are built into the annuity calculations. However, these calculations are more complex. For the sake of simplicity, use a higher initial lump sum, and plan on reinvesting the surplus to cover the anticipated deficit in later years.

Your results using these rough tools will not be precise. They will merely provide a guide in the form of a range of figures. However, since there are so many uncertain variables involved, this can be a practical approach. It can provide you with a snapshot of where you are and where you are going as you monitor your net worth growth annually. Update these retirement planning calculations every couple of years, or whenever one of the variables changes or becomes obvious.

Appendix I

Sample Financial Plan

Joanne B.

Profile: Joanne is a 40-year-old school teacher. She earns approximately $33,000 per year and has been teaching for 12 years. She is single and has no dependents. She describes herself as an aggressive saver (she saves 27% of her gross income). She states she is comfortable with a moderate degree of risk in her investments. She wants to retire completely in 15 years at age 55, and wants to travel extensively.

Investments: Joanne saves and invests $9,000 per year. She purchased a condominium as a personal residence seven years ago. She refinanced the condo three years ago with a fixed rate, fifteen-year mortgage. She makes no mortgage principal prepayment for the following reasons:

1. She has a 15-year mortgage and will own her residence free and clear in 12 years with no prepayment.
2. Her equity in the condo is a large 34% of her investment assets.
3. She has a below market rate on her loan.
4. She has a large bond asset allocation.

She has $5000/year deducted from her salary and invested via her tax deferred 403B plan. She has made this contribution each of the past ten years. This contribution lowers her reported income and thus saves her approximately $1600 in taxes each year. $192 is automatically deducted from each biweekly paycheck and *dollar-cost averaged* into a no load stock mutual fund within the 403B plan.

She contributes $2000 each January to her IRA by purchasing a new U.S. Treasury STRIP zero coupon bond. All *zeroes* are purchased to mature at age 59 1/2 or 60. It is a self-directed IRA at a discount broker.

She also purchases United States EE Savings Bonds ($1000 year) via monthly $83 purchases.

The remaining $1000 of her $9000 yearly investment goes to a money market mutual fund ($83 per month).

Her investment net worth is currently $218,000. Financial assets are invested close to a 60-30-10 ratio (they are 61%-25%-13%). New money is invested in a 56%-33%-11% ratio. (See asset lists below).

Tax Planning: Her tax planning is integrated into her permanent investment plan via her two tax deferred plans and the preferential tax treatment of her condominium. If her stock mutual fund and zero coupon bonds were in taxable accounts, her yearly tax bill would be sharply higher. She plans to continue making her annual IRA contribution regardless of deductibility. Interest on savings bonds is tax deferred.

Retirement Planning: She spends little now, but wishes to travel extensively during retirement. This would require an income equal to or greater than her current income (in today's dollars). She has never paid FICA taxes, and will receive no social security benefit. She and her financial planner estimate her average portfolio return will be approximately 10%, and they estimate she will need approximately $700,000 to generate enough income for the remainder of her life. They estimate that her current $143,000 of financial assets plus an additional $9,000 per year will grow to approximately $900,000 in fifteen years. She will continue with her current program to provide a cushion or margin for error, but will reevaluate in two or three years. At that time, she may decrease savings and increase current spending. In either case, her goal seems easily obtainable at this point.

Assets:

Money Market Mutual Fund	$19,000	9%
Stock Mutual Fund	87,700	40%
U.S. EE Savings Bonds	17,600	8%
U.S. Treasury STRIP Zero Coupon Bonds	18,700	9%
Equity in Principal Residence	<u>75,000</u>	<u>34%</u>
	218,000	100%

All Assets by Category

Equities

    Stock Mutual Fund $87,700   40%

Bonds:

    U.S. Treasury STRIP Zero
        Coupon Bonds $18,700
    U.S. EE Savings Bonds   <u>17,600</u>
                                   $36,300   17%

Real Estate:

    Equity in residence $75,000   34%

Cash:

    Money Market Mutual Fund $19,000   9%
                                           =====
                                           $218,000   100%

Financial Assets by Category
(real estate excluded)

Stocks	$ 87,700	61%
Bonds	36,300	25%
Cash	<u>19,000</u>	13%
	$143,000	

New Money ($9,000 per year)

Stocks	$ 5,000	56%
Bonds	3,000	33%
Cash	<u>1,000</u>	11%
	$ 9,000	

Appendix II

Basic Recommended Reading List

This list has been prepared to assist investors who want to take charge of their financial affairs. It is not intended to be all-inclusive. Rather, I have attempted to compile a list of sources which provide simple, concise, credible, relevant, and unbiased information.

The list includes books, periodicals, pamphlets, booklets, and newsletters.

I strongly urge investors to disregard junk mail solicitations for subscriptions to newsletters promising huge profits, market timing methods, economic predictions, and tax reduction methods. They are inappropriate for most investors, especially for those building a basic portfolio.

Basic Recommended Reading List

Topic: **Basic General Planning**

* 1. "12 Steps to Financial Security", (article), *Money Magazine* - January, 1988.
* 2. *Price Waterhouse Book of Personal Financial Planning*, Stanley Breitbard - Henry Holt & Co. - 1988 (Part 1).

Topic: **Investment Principles**

*1. "Value Spoken Here", (article), *Forbes Magazine*, June 27, 1988.
*2. *American Association of Individual Investors*, (newsletter), 625 N. Michigan Avenue, Chicago, IL 60611. ($49 per year)
*3. *The Only Other Investment Guide You'll Ever Need*, Andrew Tobias, Bantam Book, 1989.
*4. "The Dollar Cost Averaging Advantage", (pamphlet), available from Vanguard Financial Center, Valley Forge, PA 19482.

*5. *Price Waterhouse Book of Personal Financial Planning*,
Stanley Breitbard, Henry Holt & Co.,1988, (Part II).

6. *Dun and Bradstreet's Guide to Your Investments 1989*,
Nancy Dunnan, Harper & Row, ($10.95).

Topic: **Mutual Funds**

*1. *Forbes Magazine*, "Annual Mutual Fund Survey",
(September).

* 2. *Individual Investor's Guide to No-Load Mutual Funds*,
(annual). Send $5 to: Mutual Fund Education Alliance,
P.O. Box 11162, Chicago, IL 60611.

* 3. *Handbook for No-Load Fund Investors*, (annual),
Sheldon Jacobs. Send $38 to: The No-Load Fund Investor,
P.O. Box 283, Hastings-on-Hudson, New York 10706.

4. *Barron's Magazine*, (Quarterly mutual fund survey).

Topic: **United States Treasury Securities**

* 1. *Buying Federal Treasury Securities at Federal Reserve Banks*,
(booklet). Send $4.50 to: Federal Reserve Bank of Richmond,
Box 27471, Richmond, VA.

(Information is included on both Series EE Savings Bonds for my basic plan as well as United States Treasury Notes for my secondary strategy.)

Topic: **Miscellaneous**

1. *Your Money Personality*
Kathleen Gurney, Doubleday, 1988.

2. *A Banker's Secret*
Marc Eisenson, Good Advice Press, Box 78,
Elizaville, NY 12523 ($4.95)
(Subject: Prepayment of mortgage principal).

3. *Life Insurance: A Consumer's Handbook*
Joseph Belth, Indiana University Press, 1985.

Appendix III

Value of $10,000 Lump Sum invested at 10% Compound Annual Return

End of Year	Amount
1	$ 11,000
5	16,105
10	25,937
15	41,772
20	67,275
25	108,347

Appendix IV

Value of $1,000 Per Year Compounded Annually at 10%

End of Year	Amount
1	$ 1,100
5	6,716
10	17,531
15	34,950
20	63,003
25	108,182

(To calculate larger amounts, round off to thousands and multiply. Example: $5,000 per year [round off to 5] invested for 15 years = 5 X $34,950 or $174,750.)

Appendix V

Secondary Strategy: Stock Market Valuation

A. Historic Range of Dividend Yield on S & P 500 Stocks

    Low: Below 3% (overvalued stock market)
    Average: 3% to 6%
    High: Above 6% (undervalued stock market)

B. Historic Range of Price/Earnings Ratio on S & P 500 Stocks

    Low: 10 or less (undervalued stock market)
    Average: 11 to 18
    High: over 18 (overvalued stock market)

Appendix VI

Tax Deferral Advantage

Twenty year investment of $10,000 lump sum at 12% compound rate of return (33% tax bracket)

1. Within deferred account:

$96,463	at end of period
-10,000	initial investment
$86,463	earnings
x .33	tax bracket

   results in $28,533   taxes paid (at withdrawal)

$96,463	earnings plus $10,000 initial investment
-28,533	taxes
$67,930	net after taxes

2. Within taxable account:

   Effective yield is reduced to 8%. This is because approximately 33% of the 12% annual yield is paid in taxes each year. $10,000 lump sum invested for 20 years at 8% compound annual return equals:

   $46,609   net after taxes.

Appendix VII

Investment Net Worth/Asset Allocation Statement

Monitoring your progress is crucial. I have developed the following combination investment net worth and asset allocation statement to enable investors to do this themselves.

Note that I have excluded all non-investment assets and property from this statement. This will enable you to focus on building net worth. Although the personal residence can be considered as an investment, I have excluded it also.

For purposes of this statement, do not categorize assets in terms of tax treatment (taxable, tax deferred, or tax free). List all investment assets in generic terms whether they are in IRA, Keogh, 401K, or ordinary taxable accounts.

Be careful if you use computer software for net worth monitoring. Some programs I have seen use formats which can give misleading results.

I recommend that a new statement be completed each calendar quarter (or at least every six months). The statement will show your current investment net worth, how much it has increased over the last quarter, and whether you are on target toward the annual compound rate of return necessary to achieve your goals. It will also indicate whether your asset allocation is in line with your plan's recommended allocation. It should take about one to two hours to complete.

Date: _____

Investment Net Worth/Asset Allocation Statement

Cash

Bank Accounts _____
Credit Union Accounts _____
Money Market Mutual Funds _____
Bank Money Market Funds _____
Accounts Receivable _____
Insurance Cash Value _____
CD's (less than one year maturity) _____
Other _____
_____

    Cash Total _____ Percentage_____

Bonds/Notes

U.S. Treasury Notes _____
U.S. EE Savings Bonds _____
U.S. Treasury Zero Coupon Bonds _____
Government Bonds/Mutual Funds _____
Corporate Bonds/Mutual Funds _____
GNMA Mutual Funds _____
Bond Portion of Balanced
 Mutual Fund _____
Fixed Annuity _____
CD's (one year or more maturity) _____
Guaranteed Investment Contract _____
Other _____
_____

    Bond/Note Total _____ Percentage_____

Stocks

Individual Stocks _____
Stock Mutual Funds _____
Stock Portion of Balanced
   Mutual Funds _____
Stock Options _____
Other _____
   _____

        Stock Total _____ Percentage _____

Precious Metals

Gold/Silver Bullion (or coins) _____
Gold Mutual Funds _____
Other _____
   _____

        Metals Total _____ Percentage _____

Equity in Investment Real Estate (residence excluded)

Limited Partnership (cost) _____
Property 1 _____
Property 2 _____
REIT'S _____

        R.E. Total _____ Percentage _____

Collectibles

_____

_____

        Collectible Total _____ Percentage _____

Investment Asset Total	_____
Minus Liabilities	_____
Investment Net Worth	_____
Minus Last Quarter Total	_____
Quarterly Increase in Investment Net Worth	_____
Minus New Money Added	_____
Net Quarterly Increase	_____
Quarterly % Increase	_____
Annual % Increase	_____

To prepare the statement, follow these directions:

General:

You will need a business calculator, a current newspaper business section (or *Barrons* or *Wall Street Journal* and copies of all your latest investment statements. If you own investment real estate, you will also need loan balances and current market value. Exclude your personal residence, as well as non-investment assets such as cars, furniture, jewelry, etc.

Cash:

Use statements for balances. Call your insurance company for cash value of policy, if necessary.

Bonds/Notes:

1. The value of your EE Savings Bonds is their cost at the onset plus accumulated interest. Interest earned is adjusted semiannually at 85% of the five-year treasury note rate. First call 415/974-2330 to obtain the current rate. Then use your business calculator to calculate current value. For example, if your cost was $1,000 for

bonds in January and the rate was 7.5% for the six-month period, your bonds are worth $1,019 on your April 1st quarterly net worth statement.

2. Calculate the current value of your U.S. Treasury STRIP zero coupon bond in much the same way. Use the coupon rate (which stays constant). For example, if you purchased $2,000 of twenty-year *zeroes* in your IRA account, they would be worth approximately $2340, two years later if they had a 9% coupon rate. (It would vary slightly with different commission charges.) Note that your monthly statement will show **market value** which could be much different. Disregard since you should hold the bonds to maturity.

3. Statements containing investments in Bonds, Bond Mutual Funds, and GNMA Mutual Funds often show current value. If not, locate current net asset value of fund in newspaper, and multiply this times total number of shares owned from statement to get current value.

4. If you own a Balanced Mutual Fund, you should be aware of what proportion is invested in bonds. This is usually a fixed percentage (say 30-40%). Multiply this percentage times the total fund value to get the value of the bond holdings for your statement. This is essential for proper allocation monitoring. If you list 100% of a balanced fund as a stock investment, your asset allocation cannot be determined properly.

5. Insurance products (such as fixed annuities) are harder to value. If you do not have an up-to-date statement, call the insurance company or estimate current value with your calculator. Universal life and single premium life products are extremely difficult to monitor and value. This is one of many reasons I advise avoiding them.

Stocks

1. Stocks and Stock Mutual Funds can be valued using statements and current quotes from the newspaper.

2. Calculate the value of the stock portion of the balanced mutual fund just as the bond portion was calculated.

Precious Metals:

Use the spot price of bullion quoted in the daily financial press times the number of ounces you own.

Equity in Investment Real Estate:

1. If you own real estate limited partnerships, use your cost. Current value is very difficult to estimate.

2. List equity in each property only (current market value minus mortgage debt).

3. REITS trade as stocks and can be valued in the same manner.

Collectibles:

List only *wholesale* value of investment grade collectibles. Retail price is usually unattainable should you sell. Examples are numismatic coins, top grade classic autos, certain types of fine art, etc. They must be graded and appraised.

Liabilities:

Total any vehicle loans, credit card debt, and personal loans. Include home equity loans and any second mortgages unless they were taken out when you purchased your residence. This total will reflect your consumer debt.

Appendix VIII

Term Life Insurance

Quote Services:

    1. Selectquote 1-800/343-1985
    2. Insurance Quote 1-800/972-1104
    3. Life Quote 1-800/521-7873

Companies:

    USAA 1-800/531-8000
    Ameritas Life 1-800/255-9678